FORGOTTEN VOICES OF THE GREAT WAR

FORGOTTEN VOICES OF THE GREAT WAR

IN ASSOCIATION WITH THE

IMPERIAL WAR MUSEUM

MAX ARTHUR

EBURY PRESS
LONDON

First published in Great Britain in 2006

1 3 5 7 9 10 8 6 4 2

Text © Max Arthur and The Imperial War Museum 2006
Photographs © The Imperial War Museum 2006 (*see* p.160 for picture credits).
Maps by Rodney Paull

First published by Ebury Publishing
Random House, 20 Vauxhall Bridge Road, London SW1V 2SA

Random House Australia (Pty) Limited
20 Alfred Street, Milsons Point, Sydney, New South Wales 2061, Australia

Random House New Zealand Limited
18 Poland Road, Glenfield, Auckland 10, New Zealand

Random House South Africa (Pty) Limited
Isle of Houghton, Houghton, 2198, South Africa

The Random House Group Limited Reg. No. 954009

www.randomhouse.co.uk

A CIP catalogue record for this book is available from the British Library.

Editor: Amanda Li
Designer: David Fordham

ISBN 009191227X
ISBN-13 [from January 2007] 9780091912277

Papers used by Ebury Press are natural, recyclable products made from wood grown in sustainable forests.

Printed and bound in Singapore by Tien Wah Press

PREVIOUS PAGE: *Reconstruction of a soldier in a trench.*

RIGHT: *This poster emphasises the success of the newly formed Royal Air Force (April 1918), and calls for volunteers.*

NOTE: Some of the following accounts contain weights and measurements in the Imperial system, which was in use at the time of the First World War. Here is a conversion table that shows the approximate metric equivalents:

DISTANCE
1 inch = 2.5 centimetres
1 foot = 30 centimetres
1 yard = 0.9 metres
1 mile = 1.6 kilometres

WEIGHT
1 pound (abbreviated as 'lb.') = 0.4 kilogrammes
1 hundredweight = 50 kilogrammes

CONTENTS

1 WAR BREAKS OUT

WAR TALK 24
How people felt about the impending war

BECOMING A SOLDIER 29
Young men's stories of enlistment and military training

THE FIGHTING BEGINS 38
Travelling to the action and the first outbreaks of fighting

2 THE GREAT WAR

3 THE FINAL MONTHS

ACKNOWLEDGEMENTS

I WISH TO THANK Christopher Dowling, the former Director of Public Services at the Imperial War Museum, who originally offered me this challenging project and gave me wholehearted support. Within the Imperial War Museum I am indebted to Margaret Brooks, the Keeper of the Sound Archive, and her excellent staff. I must also thank the Imperial War Museum's historian Terry Charman for his valuable contribution to the book, and Liz Bowers for all her help.

At my publishers Ebury Press I owe a debt to Carey Smith, my editor, who has been a tower of strength. She has been ably supported by her editorial assistant, the extremely helpful Natalie Hunt. My agent, Barbara Levy, who is also the agent for the Imperial War Museum, helped create the project and has been a hundred per cent behind it throughout and I thank her.

PREFACE
to the Original Edition

Forgotten Voices of the Great War has been created entirely from the remarkable collection of taped interviews held by the Sound Archive of the Imperial War Museum. It is an archive of extraordinary depth, containing thousands of taped recordings of men and women who have served or witnessed the wars and campaigns from the First World War to the present. I have drawn extensively from these interviews listening to hundreds of hours of tapes and reading countless transcripts.

Although the First World War involved many countries, I have concentrated on the Western Front and the Gallipoli Campaign. Throughout the book, wherever possible I have sought to use the rank or job description held at the time. Some may register as a private but later progress to a NCO or a commission, others may change their job. It was not always possible to identify each individual's regiment.

Recalling experiences forty or fifty years after the event can lead to recollections that are understandably not always accurate in every single detail, but what cannot be taken away is the feeling that comes from these interviews and I have tried to capture this intensity. It has been a privilege to listen to the voices of the men and women, many now long dead, and to try to bring to life again their vivid memories. These are their words – I have been but a catalyst.

Max Arthur

About the First World War

'Well, a lot of people thought it would be over by Christmas. I was never one of those.'

Private Tom Adlam, 4th battalion, Hampshire Regiment

In the summer of 1914, war broke out in Europe. In the early days, most people believed the fighting would last for just a few months. They were proved wrong. The war continued for four long years.

Nobody could have imagined then that so many lives would be lost. By the end of the war, in 1918, an estimated 21 million people had been killed.

The First World War was more than anyone could have foreseen. Not only was it a longer and more devastating war than people had believed possible, it was a very different kind of war to previous conflicts. Armies had to use strategies that were completely new to them. On the battlefield, many inventions and technologies made their first appearance, from the use of radio communication to the first attack of deadly poison gas. The war also affected those at home much more than in past conflicts, with civilians being bombed and killed. Food shortages and rationing made everyday life hard. And when it was finally over, the war left a long-lasting impact on society, both on the people at 'the home front' and on the soldiers who survived it.

Left: One of many posters appealing to women to join the services and do their bit. This one is from 1917.

WHY DID THE FIRST WORLD WAR HAPPEN?

The reasons for the 'Great War', as it is still known, are complex and continue being debated even to this day. In fact, the story behind this conflict goes back long before 1914. Since the late nineteenth century, there had been an ongoing struggle and increasing tension between the main European powers. Arms races and fierce competition in trade and in the rush to gain new colonies around the world, had led to hostility and suspicion between many countries. Two of the great powers of the time, Austria–Hungary and Russia, were clashing with each other for influence in the Balkan states of south-eastern Europe. Germany was challenging the supremacy of the British Navy, the most powerful fleet in the world at that time. And Germany's ruler, Kaiser Wilhelm II, was pursuing an aggressive foreign policy, which created suspicion and mistrust in the rest of Europe.

In this tense atmosphere European countries looked to each other to make strategic alliances that would help them become more powerful. In the early part of the century, many treaties and agreements were made between the various powers, with the result that by 1914, Europe was divided into two mighty military alliances (see map, opposite).

Europe in December 1914

Allies
Central Powers
Neutral

0   300 miles
0   400 kilometres

NORWAY
SWEDEN
UNITED KINGDOM
DENMARK
RUSSIA
NETHER-LANDS
BELGIUM
LUX
GERMAN EMPIRE
FRANCE
SWITZER-LAND
AUSTRO-HUNGARIAN EMPIRE
ROUMANIA
Black Sea
PORTUGAL
SPAIN
ITALY
MONTE-NEGRO
SERBIA
BULGARIA
ALBANIA
GREECE
OTTOMAN EMPIRE
Mediterranean Sea
MOROCCO
ALGERIA

THE CENTRAL POWERS: GERMANY, AUSTRIA–HUNGARY AND ITALY

(TURKEY ALSO SIGNED A SECRET ALLIANCE WITH GERMANY IN AUGUST 1914.
BULGARIA JOINED THE CENTRAL POWERS IN 1915.)

THE TRIPLE ENTENTE (KNOWN AS THE ALLIES): FRANCE, GREAT BRITAIN AND RUSSIA

COUNTRIES THAT LATER JOINED THE ALLIES: ITALY (1915), PORTUGAL (1916),
ROMANIA (1916), GREECE (1917).

SOME COUNTRIES, SUCH AS THE NETHERLANDS AND SPAIN, REMAINED NEUTRAL.

Looking at the 1914 map you can see that this was a very different Europe to the one we know today. At its heart was the empire of Austria–Hungary, which stretched across central Europe. The Austro–Hungarian Empire included many peoples, some of whom wanted their independence, or to join other independent countries. Bosnia was one such country. It had been part of Austria–Hungary since 1908 but adjoining Serbia wanted to expand and take Bosnia over. Austria–Hungary was desperate to keep control in the Balkan region, fearful that its powerful rival, Russia, would gain a foothold here. It was in this climate that a group of Serbian nationalists formed a secret society called the Black Hand, a gang who were responsible for firing what were later called 'the first shots of the war'.

WHO WAS FRANZ FERDINAND?

The ruling emperor of Austria–Hungary had a nephew, Archduke Franz Ferdinand, who was the heir to the Austro–Hungarian Empire. On 28 June, 1914, Ferdinand was visiting Sarajevo, Bosnia, when a Black Hand member jumped on to his open car, firing two shots. The archduke and his wife were killed and the assassination sparked a chain of events that led to full-scale war.

Austria–Hungary blamed Serbia for Franz Ferdinand's death and, shortly after issuing an ultimatum, declared war on Serbia, on 28 July. It was then that the alliance system came into play. As each declaration of war was made, more countries found themselves drawn into war through the alliances they had formed in previous years.

Russia supported Serbia. Germany, allied to Austria–Hungary, declared war on Russia, then on France.

To avoid fighting a war on two fronts – against Russia in the east and France in the west – the Germans sprang into action. They would attack France first and eliminate one of their enemies. So they invaded Belgium, a neutral country, to get to France. Britain, bound by a treaty to defend Belgium, declared war on Germany.

Gradually, other countries across the world, many of which were colonies and dominions of the European powers, became participants in the war.

And so it was that within four and a half weeks of one man's assassination, what had begun as a limited conflict in central Europe had escalated into a global war.

ABOVE: *Archduke Franz Ferdinand and his wife about to enter their car, shortly before they were assassinated.*

A Short History of the War

1914

IN AUGUST, THE BRITISH EXPEDITIONARY FORCE ARRIVED IN FRANCE AND fought its first battle against the Germans at Mons. The Germans then came very close to capturing Paris but were halted by the Allies at the Battle of the Marne in September.

The German strategy was to advance in a huge outflanking movement, sweeping through Belgium and into France. As each army tried to outflank the other, a 'race to the sea' developed and trenches were dug by both sides.

RIGHT: *Keeping his head down, a soldier of the Honourable Artillery Company peers through a box periscope at enemy trenches.*

The war gathered pace further when Japan joined the Allies and the Ottoman Empire (Turkey) joined the Central Powers. Naval warfare got underway and British warships blockaded Germany. By the end of the year, British North Sea coastal towns had been bombarded by German warships.

1915

As the new year dawned, it became clear that the war would not be over quickly. On the Western Front, the Allies had some limited success in various battles and assaults, but little ground was gained by either side. There were, however, huge numbers of casualties and more volunteers had to be brought in by both sides. Poison gas was used by the Germans for the first time in April.

At sea, the British naval fleet again blockaded German ports, leading to food shortages and riots in Germany. Germany announced unrestricted submarine warfare and blockaded Britain. Then, in May, the passenger ship, SS *Lusitania*, was torpedoed by a German submarine, just off the coast of Ireland. Of the 1,200 people who drowned, 128 were US citizens. Public opinion in the United States, which had declared itself neutral, began to turn against Germany.

Further afield, Britain and France attempted to defeat the Ottoman Empire by launching an attack on the Dardanelles. The failed attempt led to the Allies trying to open a new front in Turkey, making the Gallipoli landings of 25 April in which British, Australian, New Zealand, Indian and French forces took part. The battered Allies were eventually forced to withdraw in early 1916.

On the Eastern and Balkan Fronts, fierce fighting continued as the Central Powers attacked Russia and Serbia.

THE ZEPPELINS ARRIVE

On the home front, in January 1915, the very first Zeppelins dropped their bombs on the east coast of England. Named after Count Zeppelin, the German who designed them, these airships were gas-fuelled and looked like giant cigar-shaped balloons. They targeted London and other British cities, killing 557 civilians but wounding many more. In total, 1,500 British civilians were killed by Zeppelins in air attacks.

ABOVE: *H. G. Wells described the obliteration of entire fleets and cities by airship attack in* The War in the Air *(1908). These airships menaced England, inflicting many casualties.*

1916

THIS YEAR SAW SOME OF THE WORST BLOODSHED OF THE WAR, WITH OVER A million dead and wounded in ten months (both sides combined).

In February the Germans began a huge attack at Verdun. The French and British pushed back at the Somme in July and this led to the most costly battle of the war in the west, in which soldiers were killed on an unprecedented scale. By the end of the first day, the British had suffered approximately 60,000 casualties, a third of whom were killed. This was the highest number of men the British Army had ever lost in a single day. The battle continued from 1 July to

18 November, but by its end, the Allies had only gained nine kilometres of German-held territory. It was at the Somme that tanks were used by the British for the first time.

In May, a significant sea battle took place between Britain and Germany in the North Sea, off the coast of Jutland, Denmark. The battle itself had no conclusive outcome but the long-term effects were very important. Even though the British had lost more men and ships, the German fleet was weakened and remained in port for the rest of the war. The British Navy had gained the upper hand and kept control in the North Sea and the English Channel. Allied supplies and troops could reach Europe more easily.

The British government introduced conscription for all men aged 18–41.

1917

THIS YEAR SAW SIGNIFICANT CHANGES IN THE EVENTS OF THE WAR. IN EASTERN Europe, the success of the German armies contributed to two revolutions in Russia, after the second of which Russia made peace with the Central Powers. An armistice was declared between them in December. Germany was then able to focus most of its efforts on the Western Front, where fierce fighting and much loss of life continued. At the Third Battle of Ypres (also known as Passchendaele) in July, many men and horses drowned in the mud.

LEFT: *Troops advancing during the Battle of the Somme, 1916.*

RIGHT: *A rather lighthearted poster disguising the reality of war at the Front.*

In early 1917 the Germans launched an all-out submarine attack on Britain, which meant that food supplies became low in Britain and rationing was introduced. However, Germany's declaration of unrestricted submarine warfare led to the United States declaring war in April. With American support, the war began to turn in the Allies' favour.

Allied forces also began to gain strength in the Middle East, taking control of Baghdad and Jerusalem.

1918

THE FINAL YEAR OF THE WAR SAW LARGE NUMBERS OF GERMAN TROOPS (many of whom were freed up from fighting on the Eastern Front) take part in a major attack that nearly broke through the Allied lines on the Western Front. However, the Allies, joined by American troops, fought back with successful counter-attacks. By the autumn the Germans were being forced to retreat and Allied troops were able to push forward and free most of occupied France and Belgium.

One by one, the other Central Powers surrendered and at 11 am on 11 November an armistice between Germany and the Allies was signed. Fighting stopped, but it was not until June 1919 that the war was officially ended with the signing of the Treaty of Versailles.

The Consequences of the Great War

The impact of the war reverberated throughout the world for years afterwards. The most immediate effect could be seen in the cities, towns and villages around the world where so many young men who had left their homes to fight, never returned. Those soldiers who did make it back were not the same as when they had left. Many were badly injured. Most had witnessed terrible sights and suffering during their time at the Front.

During the war years, the position of women in society had changed a great deal. Huge supplies of ammunition had been desperately needed at the front and women had been called upon as workers to produce them. They had also been doing what were thought of as 'men's jobs', such as working on the land to grow crops. In Britain, women could even volunteer to work in military service for the first time when

THE TRUTH ABOUT SHELL-SHOCK

Traumatised by the horrors of the war, many former soldiers found themselves unable to cope with everyday life. The men experienced different kinds of symptoms, but common problems included nightmares, stammering or being unable to eat or sleep properly. The condition was later labelled 'shell-shock' but it wasn't until many years later that this stress-related illness was properly understood by the medical profession.

RIGHT: Many women volunteered to take over the work of farm hands who had joined up. Here, two members of the Women's Land Army are feeding a hay baler.

the government set up the Women's Auxiliary Army Corps in 1917. All in all, it isn't surprising that women felt differently about themselves and their role in society once the war was over.

In Britain, their contribution was recognised to some extent when, on 28 December, 1918, women over the age of 30 were allowed to vote for the first time. This was a huge leap forward for women.

The First World War completely changed the world and its political climate. Europe had been thrown into turmoil for four years and was now left in a state of economic and political instability, with many countries in huge debt from financing the war and with hungry populations to feed. The old empires had collapsed and a new map of Europe was slowly re-drawn as new countries appeared.

In Germany conditions were particularly bad. The terms of the Treaty of Versailles had been very harsh and had left the German people humiliated and bitter. Forced to pay huge amounts of compensation to the Allies, the country's economy was in crisis and the effects of poverty and high unemployment took their toll on the population, until, in 1932, reparations were suspended. The difficult conditions created in Germany by then had paved the way for the rise of Hitler and the Nazi Party.

1
WAR
BREAKS
OUT

LEFT: *The brutality of the Germans towards Belgian women and children provoked this poster.*

ABOVE: *A poster calling for all walks of life to enlist.*

WAR TALK

By early August 1914, there was war in Europe. People gathered in the streets to cheer on their soldiers, with thoughts of victory in their minds. Amongst the men there was no shortage of willing recruits – most believed the war would be over within a few months.

BELOW LEFT: *French troops on their way to the Front.*

RIGHT: *A sergeant measuring recruits for their uniforms.*

Private Tom Adlam
4th Battalion, Hampshire Regiment

'WELL, A LOT OF PEOPLE THOUGHT IT WOULD BE OVER BY CHRISTMAS. I was never one of those who thought that at the beginning. But I put it down for about a year. I think most of us thought it would last about a year. We thought it couldn't go on longer than that. '

Elizabeth Owen
English schoolgirl

'I WAS SEVEN AND I WAS PLAYING IN THE GARDEN WHEN I WAS ASKED TO go and speak to my grandmother. She said, 'Now children, I have got something very serious to tell you. The Germans are fighting the British, there is a war on and all sorts of people will be killed by these wicked Germans. And therefore there must be no playing, no singing and no running about.' And then she took from us all our toys that were made in Germany, amongst them a camel of which I was very fond. '

Bands playing, flags flying, a terrific sort of overwhelming conviction that Germany now would go into war and win it very quickly.

MY MEMORIES ARE THOSE OF A child of course. I was in a small German garrison town in 1914 and I remember very well the tremendous enthusiasm. Of course, we schoolboys were all indoctrinated with great patriotism when war broke out. My father was an active infantry officer and I shall never forget the day when they marched out to the trains. All the soldiers were decorated with flowers, there was no gun which did not show a flower. Even the horses, I think, were decorated. And of course all the people followed them. Bands playing, flags flying, a terrific sort of overwhelming conviction that Germany now would go into war and win it very quickly.

WE HAD BEEN ON HOLIDAY IN FRANCE FOR TEN DAYS. ALTHOUGH THERE had been rumours of war, my father didn't believe them. But then war broke out, so we made our way to Le Havre by boat. We went to a hotel, had a clean-up and then went out in the town and then the excitement began. It was absolutely

ABOVE: *Young German recruits prepare to leave for the Front in 1914 with their helmets decorated with flowers and ribbons.*

The soldiers were marching in, all singing.

incredible. The British Expeditionary Force was coming in. The soldiers were marching in, all singing. French people, all excited, madly waving, dashing about and rushing up to the soldiers, pulling off their buttons as keepsakes, kissing them and – oh! – terrific excitement! It was marvellous that here they were. So we stayed there during the day and then we got the boat to Southampton at night. We arrived in the early hours of the morning and went up to London and there the contrast was incredible. From the excitement in France to the gloom of London. Everybody there with long faces and an 'Oh, isn't it terrible' sort of attitude. You could hardly believe it was possible, that there was such a change from the two sides of the Channel.

Robert Poustis
French student

"IN THE FIRST DAYS OF MOBILISATION THERE WAS, OF COURSE, A LOT OF enthusiasm. Everybody was shouting and wanted to go to the Front. The cars, the railway wagons loaded with soldiers were full of tricolour flags and inscriptions: 'À Berlin, à Berlin.' We wanted to go to Berlin immediately, with bayonets, swords and lances, running after the Germans. The war, we thought, was to last two months, maybe three months."

Captain Philip Neame VC
15th Field Company, Royal Engineers

"I WAS STATIONED AT GIBRALTAR WHEN WAR was declared, and we officers there were afraid that the war would be over quickly, and that we should miss it because we were not part of the British Expeditionary Force. We were all keen soldiers, and if there was a war in which the British Army was taking part we were all only too anxious to be at the Front."

THE BRITISH EXPEDITIONARY FORCE (BEF)

The first British soldiers to arrive in France were the BEF, known as 'The Old Contemptibles'. The nickname came from the German kaiser – who had supposedly described them as 'that contemptible little army'. The BEF were regular soldiers who confronted the Germans at the Battle of Mons on 23 August, before being forced to retreat.

BECOMING A SOLDIER

In August 1914, Lord Kitchener, the Secretary of State for War, asked for 100,000 volunteers to join the British Army. Men queued up to enlist, even though many were not yet nineteen, the minimum age requirement for the British army to serve overseas at this time.

Private Reginald Haine
1st Battalion, Honourable Artillery Company

'M Y FIRST REACTION TO THE OUTBREAK OF WAR WAS MORE OR LESS A blank, because I really did not think much about it. I was only just eighteen, and right at the start I didn't think that it would affect me to any extent. I was an articled clerk to a firm of chartered accountants and I was due for a fortnight's holiday. I went on that holiday on August the 4th.

When I came back I went back to the office on the Monday morning and a friend of mine phoned me and said, 'What are you doing about the war?' Well, I had thought nothing about it at all. He said, 'Well, I have joined my brother's regiment which is the Honourable Artillery Company. If you like, come along, I can get you in.'

At lunchtime I left the office, in Southampton Row, went along to Armoury House, in the City Road, and there was my friend waiting for me. There was a queue of about a thousand people trying to enlist at the time, all in the HAC – it

BELOW LEFT: *Young recruits taking the oath.*

RIGHT: *Volunteers at Central Recruiting Office, Great Scotland Yard, London.*

went right down City Road. But my friend came along the queue and pulled me out of it and said, 'Come along!' So I went right up to the front, where I was met by a sergeant-major at a desk. My friend introduced me to the sergeant, who said, 'Are you willing to join?' I said, 'Yes Sir.' He said, 'Well, how old are you?' I said, 'I am eighteen and one month.' He said, 'Do you mean nineteen and one month?' So I thought a moment and said, 'Yes Sir.' He said, 'Right-ho, well sign here please.' He said, 'You realise you can go overseas?' So that was my introduction to the Army.

There was a queue of about a thousand people trying to enlist at the time, all in the HAC – it went right down City Road.

KITCHENER'S NEW ARMIES

Lord Kitchener's face appeared on recruiting posters all over the country, urging men to enlist. Fighting for your country was seen to be a glorious and patriotic duty and many British men rose to the challenge. Half a million men volunteered within a few weeks of Britain going to war.

Private Thomas McIndoe
12th Battalion, Middlesex Regiment

6 It was seeing the picture of Kitchener and his finger pointing at you – any position that you took up the finger was always pointing to you – it was a wonderful poster really.

I was always a tall and fairly fit lad. When I confronted the recruiting officer he said that I was too young, although I had said that I was eighteen years of age. He said, 'Well, I think you are too young son. Come back in another year or so.' I returned home and never said anything to my parents. I picked up my bowler hat, which my mother had bought me and which was only to wear on Sundays, and I donned that thinking it would make me look older. I presented myself to the recruiting officer again, and this time there was no queries, I was accepted. Birth certificates were not asked for, although I had one, not with me but I had one. My mother was very hurt when I arrived home that night and told her that I had to report to Mill Hill next morning. I was sixteen in the June. **9**

Marjorie Llewellyn
English schoolgirl

6 As a young schoolgirl I remember there was great excitement in Sheffield when the posters went up showing Kitchener saying 'We Want You' and a number of our young men joined up – they were the pick of the city. They were highly educated, most of them, what was called the officer class. And they went to the Town Hall, signed on, and then to their great disappointment were sent home again. This of course was very unexpected. They had expected to be in uniform straight away and rush off to win the war, which of course everyone

RIGHT: *The image of the stern and unforgiving face of Lord Kitchener is probably the most famous poster of the Great War.*

ABOVE: *New recruits learning to march in Hyde Park, London, shortly after war had been declared in August 1914.*

thought would be over by Christmas. However, they had to go each day to the drill hall and sign on again. Then they were sent down to the Bramall Lane Football Ground and to Norfolk Park, where they were drilled and learned to dig trenches, and this went on for quite a long time. They felt they were playing at soldiers, not really doing what they intended. However, soon they were put into a camp a short distance out of the town and there their training began in earnest. ''

FRONT-LINE FRIENDS

Groups of friends and people who worked together were encouraged to enlist at the same time and form what were called 'Pals' battalions, with names like the 'Grimsby Chums', 'Newcastle Commercials' or the 'Glasgow Tramways Battalion'. As a consequence, during the course of the war, some towns and villages lost almost all their young men.

Corporal Stefan Westmann
29th Division, German Army

"I WAS A MEDICAL STUDENT WHEN I RECEIVED MY CALL-UP PAPERS. THEY ordered me to report for military duty in a clean state and free of vermin at an infantry regiment in Freiburg, in Baden. We had no idea of any impending war, we had no idea that the danger of war existed. We served in our blue-and-red uniform, but on the 1st of August mobilisation orders came and we put on our field grey. At 2 o'clock in the morning of the 4th of August we marched out of Freiburg with torches – silent, without any music, without any singing, and with no enthusiasm. We were really weighed down by our kit, which weighed 75 lb. per man. We crossed the Rhine over a very wobbly pontoon bridge into Alsace."

We were really weighed down by our kit,

which weighed 75 lb. per man.

Rifleman Henry Williamson
London Rifle Brigade

"DURING OUR TRAINING IN CROWBOROUGH IN SUSSEX IT WAS A MONTH OF great heat, we sweated tremendously. We carried about 60 lb. of ammunition, kit and our rifle. We got blisters, but we did about fifteen or sixteen miles a day, with ten minutes' halt every hour. We lay on our backs gasping, water bottles were drunk dry, people in cottages, women in sun bonnets came up with apples and jugs of water and we passed some of the battalions who had been in front of us whose headquarters were in some of the poorer quarters of London, and I remember so well the dead-white faces, many with boils, lying completely exhausted, sun-stricken in the hedges, hundreds of them."

Private S. C. Lang

"I WAS WALKING DOWN THE CAMDEN High Street when two young ladies approached and said, 'Why aren't you in the Army with the boys?' So I said, 'I'm sorry but I'm only seventeen,' and one of them said, 'Oh we've heard that one before. I suppose you're also doing work of national importance.' Then she put her hand in her bag and pulled out a feather. I raised a hand thinking she was going to strike me and this feather was pushed up my nose.

I raised a hand thinking she was going to strike me and this feather was pushed up my nose.

Then a sergeant came out of one of the shops and said to me, 'Did she call you a coward?' I said yes and felt very indignant about it. He said, 'Well, come across the road to the drill hall and we'll soon prove that you aren't a coward.' I got into the drill hall and then the sergeant said to me, 'How old are you?' I told him I was seventeen and he said, 'What did you say, nineteen?' 'No, seventeen.' 'When were you born?' '1898.' '1896?' 'No,' I said, '1898.'

He then said to me, 'Get on the scales.' He weighed me, took my height and said, 'Now we'll go round to the doctor for a medical exam.' The doctor told me to take all my clothes off, which embarrassed me very much. Any rate, I got back to the drill hall, where there were six of us waiting, and the sergeant called out my name. I walked forward and thought, 'Oh that's good, I'm not in,' and he said, 'You're the only so-and-so that's passed out of this six.'

I was astonished because I'd told him I was only seventeen and there I was, almost in the Army. I went to the recruiting office and the officer said something to me about King and country and then he said, 'Well raise your right hand and say I will,' or something like that. Then he said, 'I'm extremely sorry I haven't got your shilling, but we'll let you have that later on,' and to my amazement I found I was being called Private S. C. Lang.

Private Norman Demuth
1/5th Battalion, London Regiment

Almost the last feather I received was on a bus. I was sitting near the door when I became aware of two women on the other side talking at me, and I thought to myself, 'Oh Lord, here we go again.' I didn't pay much attention. However, I suppose I must have caught their eye in some way because one leant forward and produced a feather and said, 'Here's a gift for a brave soldier.' I took it and said, 'Thank you very much – I wanted one of those.' Then I took my pipe out of my pocket and put this feather down the stem and everything and worked it in a way I've never worked a pipe cleaner before. When it was filthy I pulled it out and said, 'You know we didn't get these in the trenches,' and handed it back to her. She instinctively put out her hand and took it, so there she was sitting with this filthy pipe cleaner in her hand and all the other people on the bus began to get indignant. Then she dropped it and got up to get out, but we were nowhere near a stopping place and the bus went on quite a long way while she got well and truly barracked by the rest of the people on the bus. I sat back and laughed like mad.

THE FIGHTING BEGINS

As the Germans advanced through Belgium and France there were heavy casualties among French and British forces. The advance was eventually stopped on the Marne. The two sides then tried to outmanoeuvre each other in a 'race to the sea'.

Western Front

— Furthest German advance 1914
— Trench warfare 1914–17
— Armistice Line 11 Nov 1918

Sergeant Stefan Westmann
29th Division, German Army

'DURING OUR ADVANCE THROUGH BELGIUM WE MARCHED ON AND ON. We never dared take off our boots, because our feet were so swollen that we didn't think it would be possible to put them on again. In one small village the mayor came and asked our company commanders not to allow us to cut off the hands of children. These were atrocity stories which he had heard about the German Army. At first we laughed about it, but when we heard of other propaganda things said against the German Army, we became angry.'

At the beginning of the war, the French army wore traditional blue jackets and distinctive, bright red trousers. This was the same uniform they had worn during the Franco–Prussian War of 1870–71, when the French army was under the command of Napoleon III. In 1915, their outfits were replaced by 'horizon blue' uniforms, which were not so conspicuous.

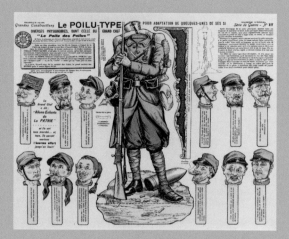

ABOVE: *A children's game showing a French soldier on which a dozen heads coud be cut out and fixed.*

Private Frank Dolbau
French Army

‘AT OUR FIRST BATTLE AT MORHANGE ON THE 19TH OF AUGUST, unsupported by artillery, against heavily fortified positions, we had attacked. We were shot down like rabbits because you know for them we were a real target, as we had red trousers on. When we were fired at we were like sitting ducks in the field, you see.’

Germaine Soltau
Belgian schoolgirl

‘I WAS IN BRUSSELS, AND AT AN AGE WHEN ALL EVENTS SEEM TO LEAVE A permanent impression on you. Of course we were not expecting the Germans to invade Belgium, we were hoping they would respect our neutrality, so the invasion came as a very great shock to us all. We had heard in Brussels what was happening at the frontier – the killing, the shooting, the atrocities and of course it was awful, but the fortresses of Liège were holding and that gave us some hope. Brussels then was very silent, and the Grande Place had never been so beautiful, with all the big flags flying on the old historical buildings. But there was much sadness and emotion.

Then on the 18th of August the government in Brussels left the capital to go to Antwerp. Soon Liège fell and the Germans were on their way to Brussels. They were preceded by streams of refugees, telling us more stories of atrocities in the villages and small towns of the Ardennes. We heard about friends from a little village – the young woman who was shot dead in front of her child just after her husband had been taken away to be shot. That happened hundreds and thousands of times, always the same story.

It was a glorious day of sunshine but in my mind I still keep a vision of grey, these grey-clad hordes marching in the streets.

Then on Thursday the 20th of August, a date I will never forget, the Germans entered Brussels. It was a glorious day of sunshine but in my mind I still keep a vision of grey, these grey-clad hordes marching in the streets. It was a sinister, greenish grey, even their helmets were covered in grey. They had with them all their heavy guns, field kitchens and officers on horseback, and it all went in long, long, endless streams of grey. And the dust that was raised by all these thousands of feet and all those weapons of war – one had the feeling that the dust was hiding the sun. And their music, the music that we were going to hear for four years and three months – the sound of drum and fife and always the same tune. It made us cry when we heard that and thought about our soldiers and of the Allies on the front line. And then in the evening, on our beautiful Grande Place, they put up their field kitchen and started making their soup.

ABOVE: *Queen's Westminster Rifles waiting for their troop train at Waterloo Station, London, during mobilisation – August 1914.*

Fusilier William Holbrook
4th Battalion, Royal Fusiliers

'THE JOURNEY ACROSS WAS PEACEFUL. WE HAD NO ESCORT, NOTHING. When we got there we camped for about three or four days then we went and trained at Le Havre, and then it was up to the Front. We went on a cattle-truck type train, eight horses and forty men. We marched from there to the Front – of course we did not know where we were going, and the whole brigade came together. We were the 9th Brigade.

Before we got to Mons we went through a place called Frameries, a mining town about ten miles from Mons. It was wonderful there, the people came out and cheered and shouted and gave us food and a tremendous welcome. '

BATTLE OF MONS
23 August 1914

This was the first battle to take place between British and German forces on the Western Front. Soldiers of the British Expeditionary Force met and fought the advancing German army at Mons in Belgium. Despite heavy losses on the German side, the British were eventually forced back to the River Marne, 48 kilometres from Paris.

Gunner Walter Burchmore
Royal Horse Artillery

'We had reached a village about three miles from Mons in our advance towards the German armies and we were enjoying the hospitality of the villagers when quite out of the blue came the order 'Prepare for Action. Get mounted.' We obeyed it immediately, rode out of the village about a couple of miles. We came into action on the high ground overlooking Mons. We immediately engaged the German artillery and that developed into a regular artillery duel in and around Binche, where we were firing in support of our infantry and cavalry who occupied it in the early morning. It was quite obvious that the Germans didn't intend to give us any rest and we quite made up our mind that we wouldn't give them any either. The infantry during the afternoon were driven out of Binche by sheer weight of numbers. Then developed quite a number of charges and counter-charges, which were very exciting and most interesting. We gave them all the support we could with our guns. We dealt very severely with a squadron of German cavalry who'd appeared on our right. We suddenly saw these people coming, didn't realise who they were at first and we said, 'By crikey! It's bloody Germans!' so we started gunfire immediately. We fired on open sights, fuse nought, and they got about two hundred yards from the guns and they

We suddenly saw these people coming, didn't realise who they were at first and we said, 'By crikey! It's bloody Germans!' so we started gunfire immediately.

wheeled to the left and galloped away to the left and rode right into a squadron of our own cavalry who dealt with them and finished where we'd left off.

Then quite suddenly we got the orders that we were going to try and retake Binche. This was in the early hours of the 24th. We did very well. The battle went on for several hours and I thought that we were going to take the place but I doubt very much whether we could have held it if we had. However, we were very disappointed when we were ordered to break up the battle and retreat. But we were thankful the Germans had withdrawn after this very severe battle because we were feeling thoroughly tired. We were completely exhausted, thoroughly hungry, and I don't think we were capable of any reasonable further movement. There was only one thing that managed to keep us going and that was the knowledge that we were fighting for our very lives.

ABOVE: *Recently arrived Belgian refugees, who were forced to leave their country with only a few possessions to seek shelter in London.*

Heinrich Beutow
German schoolboy

‘After the initial enthusiasm and patriotism came a wave of quietness, because then the first death lists were published in the papers. And my mother – she was English – was suddenly surrounded by women of the regiment, the wives of the other officers of course, and most of them – because my father's regiment was one of the first to march over the border into Belgium – were widows. And even as a child, I must say, it gave me a great shock to see that most of the officers were dead and killed during the first weeks. A lot of the younger soldiers were dead and the whole feeling of enthusiasm faded away very quickly, in my opinion. The world became grey after that. ’

A lot of the younger soldiers were dead and the whole feeling of enthusiasm faded away very quickly, in my opinion.

Gunner J. W. Palmer
Royal Field Artillery

‘After advancing several days into Belgium and passing these refugees, many of them with their little dogcarts and piled with their pitiful possessions, prams, children, one thing and another, we found ourselves eventually going the same way as the refugees, so we knew very well we were no longer advancing into Belgium. And our road got more congested with refugees and we got mixed up with the infantry, who in turn were getting more and more tired.

The infantry were carrying in the region of 100 lb. on their back, which we did not have. And so their feet got worse and worse. A lot of it was due to the fact that a number of them were reservists and had been called up just prior to the outbreak of war. They were fitted out with kit, including 'ammos' (that's the old army word for boots) and they were very heavy. Before the war we were able to break them in, but they didn't get time. They were put straight on a march which lasted for about 150, 160 miles with only a very, very few rests and if they got those boots off they couldn't get them back on again, consequently their feet were bleeding. '

BATTLE OF THE AISNE
14 – 28 September 1914

Following the Battle of the Marne, in which the Allies made a successful counter-attack against the German army, the exhausted German soldiers began to retreat. When they reached the River Aisne they stopped, dug in, and made a defensive stand, holding up firmly against Allied attacks.

BELOW: *The German army retreating from the Marne.*

At the battle of the Aisne we got over the river and onto the high ground over a mile in front of the Aisne. We knew there was about a brigade of Jerries against us and we were only seven platoons. During the fight we got pushed back about three hundred yards, we had to leave our wounded and dead. The Highland Light Infantry and Worcesters came up. Private Wilson of the HLI and or our men attacked a machine gun. Our man killed but Private Wilson killed the machine-gunner and captured the position and got the Victoria Cross. Our man got a wooden cross. That's the difference, you see. One killed – one a Victoria Cross.

ABOVE: *The Victoria Cross – the highest military award a British soldier, sailor or airman can receive. During the Great War, 634 VCs were awarded for acts of outstanding bravery.*

ARMY 'NICKNAMES'

British soldiers often used slang words for themselves, their enemies and their allies. Popular names for the Germans were 'Jerry' (or 'Jerries'), 'Fritz', 'the Boche' and 'the Hun'. British soldiers were often known as 'Tommy' while the Scots were called 'Jocks'. 'Froggies' were French soldiers.

Then the orders came through, I remember, in the tented lines on Crowborough Heath.

Rifleman Henry Williamson
London Rifle Brigade

'THEN THE ORDERS CAME THROUGH, I REMEMBER, IN THE TENTED LINES on Crowborough Heath. They came down early in the morning with the colour sergeant of the company. The fellows rolled over and kicked their legs in the air and cheered and cheered and cheered, tremendously excited. I was not excited, I was apprehensive. I did not believe the war was going to be over by Christmas, I had a feeling from having talked to chaps from Mons in the local hospital that it wasn't altogether going to be a picnic. '

First Battle of Ypres
19 October – 22 November 1914

In August the Germans had taken the Belgian town of Ypres, on the route from the Aisne to the coast. In early October, Ypres was recaptured by British forces and the Germans launched a counter-attack. In the ensuing battle the Germans, who far outnumbered the British, came close to breaking through the Allied line. When fighting ceased, there were shocking numbers of casualties on both sides, but little ground had been gained.

Private Clifford Lane
1st Battalion, Hertfordshire Regiment

'WE MOVED TO THE FRONT IN THIRTY OR FORTY LONDON OMNIBUSES. When we boarded these omnibuses everybody wanted to get on the top because it was quite a nice day, fairly bright for November. But we had not been going very long before it started to rain, so we got thoroughly soaked. We must have travelled for quite a few hours, for it was dark when we eventually reached our destination, Vlamertinge.

We were lined up and given a very generous issue of rum. I didn't even drink beer. So in no time we were quite euphoric really. We were quite happy. We did not know where we were going, but the moon broke through the clouds and it was a lovely night. And I can remember, as we marched along, we passed a Roman Catholic priest who removed his hat and murmured his blessings.

We spent a cold night in a field. In the morning we were told to go up a wooded hillside where we found dugouts. We could rest there much more

We were lined up and given a very generous issue of rum.

LEFT: *London buses transporting British troops behind the lines.*

comfortably – in a dugout you could lay down. We stayed that day, but did not go to sleep. When it was light we simply came out to survey our surroundings.

We could see a road running towards Ypres from our hillside, and on it we saw a group of French soldiers. While we were watching there was the sound of heavy gunfire and, after a few seconds, three violent explosions. When the smoke had cleared we saw this group picking up one of their number and immediately start to dig a grave for him, so the shell had killed him. That was the first time we realised what the war was about – what the Germans could do.

That was the first time we realised what the war was about – what the Germans could do.

WAR WEAPONRY

Several kinds of weapons made their first significant appearance in the First World War. Automatic weapons such as machine guns made a huge impact on the battlefield and even changed the way the war was fought. Completely new weapons, such as flamethrowers and poison gas, were to take Allied troops completely by surprise. Hand grenades, however, had existed for over 200 years but would become more sophisticated in design as the war went on. They were used by the British as early as 1914 but were extremely unpopular at first, due to their tendency to explode on contact with any object. Soldiers would often make their own grenades out of jam tins.

Captain Reginald Thomas
Royal Artillery

'WE WERE TERRIBLY SHORT OF HAND GRENADES, IN FACT I DON'T THINK they were even invented at that time. But we really needed something to hurl at the enemy. We were so close to them that occasionally we could take pot-shots, but to get something actually into a trench was a very different thing.

And so with Philip Neame's aid – he was a sapper and I was a gunner – we concocted some jam-tin bombs. I helped Neame with this little factory he was running with empty jam tins and made one or two excursions behind our lines to buy ingredients. I was able to find a shop that dealt in explosives and we got some gun-cotton and some blasting detonators. Also I was still in the mounted section, so was able to get our farriers to cut up old horseshoes and other bits of old iron to put in the bombs.

So we made these hand grenades out of jam-tin bombs and just hurled them into the German trenches. They were very successful. The War Office of the government eventually supplied us with bombs that were exactly the same shape as the jam tin – they were rather handy things to hold, you see, and you could throw them twenty or thirty yards. You couldn't have had a nicer missile to hurl. We did rather well with them.'

SAPPERS AND GUNNERS

Soldiers were often defined by the particular job they carried out during the war. A gunner, as the name suggests, is a soldier whose main responsibility is to handle and operate artillery guns. Sappers also performed an important job. One of their main tasks was to tunnel under the enemy lines and lay explosive devices, a trench strategy during the First World War. Both sides used sensitive listening devices to forewarn them of any possible underground activity.

LEFT: *A hand grenade.*

ABOVE: *Allied forces hold the German advance.
The Middlesex Regiment transport comes under fire. The
man in the centre has been badly wounded in the face.*

Sergeant Stefan Westmann
29th Division, German Army

ALL OF A SUDDEN THE ENEMY FIRE CEASED. COMPLETE SILENCE CAME over the battlefield. Then one of the chaps in my shell-hole said, 'I wonder what they are up to,' and another answered, 'Perhaps they are getting tea.' A third one said, 'Don't be a fool, do you see what I see?' And we looked over the brim of our shell-hole and there between the brick heaps, out had come a British soldier with a Red Cross flag that he waved at us. And he was followed by stretcher-bearers who came slowly towards us and collected our wounded. We got up, still completely dumb from fear of death, and helped them to bring our wounded into our trenches.

Private Frank Sumpter
London Rifle Brigade

'AFTER THE 19TH DECEMBER ATTACK, WE WERE BACK IN THE SAME trenches when Christmas Day came along. It was a terrible winter, everything was covered in snow, everything was white. The devastated landscape looked terrible in its true colours – clay and mud and broken brick – but when it was covered in snow, it was beautiful. Then we heard the Germans singing 'Silent night, Holy night', and they put up a notice saying 'Merry Christmas', so we put one up too.

DECEMBER 1914 – THE CHRISTMAS TRUCE

A surprising and memorable event took place at Christmas, 1914. Both British and German soldiers stopped firing and many were brave enough to climb out of their trenches and meet the enemy in no man's land, the devastated ground between the two front lines. They talked together, sang Christmas carols and even played football. For the first time soldiers had seen the human face of the enemy. This would never happen again on the same scale during the war.

BELOW: *During the unofficial truce at Christmas 1914, British and German troops are seen burying their dead.*

Then one German took a chance and jumped up on top of the trench and shouted out, 'Happy Christmas, Tommy!'

While they were singing our boys said, 'Let's join in,' so we joined in and when we started singing, they stopped. And when we stopped, they started again. So we were easing the way. Then one German took a chance and jumped up on top of the trench and shouted out, 'Happy Christmas, Tommy!' So of course our boys said, 'If he can do it, we can do it,' and we all jumped up. A sergeant-major shouted, 'Get down!' But we said, 'Shut up Sergeant, it's Christmas time!' And we all went forward to the barbed wire.

We could barely reach through the wire, because the barbed wire was not just one fence, it was two or three fences together, with a wire in between. And so we just shook hands and I had the experience of talking to one German who said to me, 'Do you know where the Essex Road in London is?' I replied, 'Yes, my uncles had a shoe-repairing shop there.' He said, 'That's funny. There's a barber shop on the other side where I used to work.'

They could all speak very good English because, before the war, Britain was 'invaded' by Germans. Every pork butcher was German, every barber's shop was German, and they were all over here getting the low-down on the country. It's ironic when you think about it, that he must have shaved my uncle at times and yet my bullet might have found him and his bullet might have found me.

The officers gave the order 'No fraternisation' and then they turned their backs on us. But they didn't try to stop it because they knew they couldn't. We never said a word about the war to the Germans. We spoke about our families, about how old we were, how long we thought it would last and things like that. I was young and I wasn't that interested, so I stood there for about half an hour then I came back. But most of the boys stayed there the whole day and only came back

ABOVE: *The destruction of Ypres after the battle in November.*

in the evening. There were no shots fired and some people enjoyed the curiosity of walking about in no man's land. It was good to walk around. As a sign of their friendliness the Germans put up a sign saying 'Gott mit uns', which means 'God is with us', and so we put a sign in English saying 'We got mittens too'. I don't know if they enjoyed that joke. ,

We spoke about our families, about how old we were, how long we thought it would last and things like that.

On les aura !
2E EMPRUNT
DE
LA DÉFENSE NATIONALE
Souscrivez
Y.108
DEVAMBEZ IMP PARIS

2

THE GREAT WAR

LEFT: *The famous French poster 'On les aura!' (meaning 'We'll get them!')
quotes General Philippe Pétain's words at the Battle of Verdun in 1916.*

ABOVE: *Lewis gunner in action during the Battle of the Somme.*

A Soldier's Life

The First World War was fought differently to previous wars. On the Western Front, both sides became locked in a stalemate only a few months after the war had started. With the mass use of deadly weapons such as the machine gun, it had become too dangerous for soldiers to fight in exposed areas. Trench warfare had begun.

ABOVE: *British infantry working under the guidance of the Royal Engineers in a thaw-damaged communication trench recently taken over from the French.*

Private Reginald Haine
1st Battalion, Honourable Artillery Company

‘THE FINEST TRAINING FOR WARFARE IS WARFARE ITSELF. IN A FORTNIGHT you learn more than two years of any training can teach you. And so before the end of the year we were a very seasoned battalion and – I say it without bragging – we were as good as any regular battalion in the line. There was nobody behind except people like the Army Service Corps and suppliers. But as far as the fighting troops were concerned we were all very near the front line the whole time.

TRENCH WARFARE

The trenches were intended as a temporary measure, to provide cover for the men against the fire of devastating new weaponry. As Allied and German soldiers dug those first trenches, neither side foresaw that their armies would be fighting from them for almost the entire duration of the war. It was only a matter of months before the trenches formed a continuous line, hundreds of kilometres long, stretching from the English Channel to the Franco–Swiss border. This was the Western Front. Conditions for the soldiers, who had to eat, sleep and fight from these trenches, were, at times, grim, particularly during the winter months.

ABOVE: *A short-handled trenching tool.*

Practically the whole time you had to sleep with your boots on in case things went wrong anywhere. Even if one was in support – not in reserve so much, in reserve you could get your clothes off – but if you were in support you had to sleep in your clothes. The winter of '14 was extremely hard because we had no amenities whatsoever. It was just ditches, the trenches were just waterlogged ditches, and one was often up to one's knees in frozen mud. You could do nothing about it except stick there. The actual fighting was nothing like it was in the later years of the war, the years I know most from a fighting point of view, and of course the casualties and everything then were terrific. But in '14 there were many casualties through sickness and shelling. There was shelling every day but nothing like the intensity of later on.

We had not been trained for any of the tasks we were asked to undertake. It was all improvisation really. The ordinary infanteer, he shot his rifle. And we had a couple of Vickers guns in the battalion, that's all the machine guns the battalion

*Practically the whole time
you had to sleep with your boots on
in case things went wrong
anywhere.*

had in those days. And there were specially trained people who used to have to hump up their ammunition for them, which was a hell of a job. That was because sometimes one had marched two or three miles to get near the firing line, and then we would have to carry not only our own kit with 250 rounds of ammunition, but sometimes they'd ask us to, between two people, carry up a thousand rounds of machine-gun ammunition as well. And in those conditions in the winter of '14, when everything was as muddy as it could be and there was really no drainage or anything, it was a terrific task. From a physical point of view it was a killing job but we most of us got through it. **,**

Rifleman Henry Williamson
London Rifle Brigade

It is true to say that we enjoyed our first visit to the trenches. The weather was dry, we went through a wood under Messines Hill. We were brigaded with regulars who wore balaclava helmets. The whole feeling was one of tremendous comradeship, and these old sweats who were survivors of Mons and Aisne, they had no fear at all, and any apprehension we had of going in under fire was soon got rid of in the trenches.

...we enjoyed our first visit to the trenches.

We could also go in estaminets and have omelettes, and café rum for about a halfpenny, it was great fun. We had to go on working parties at night in the woods, and then after four more nights we were in the trenches again, back slithering into the trenches and doing it all over again.

One night in the second week of November there was a tremendous storm blowing, lightning was flashing and flares were still going up. Rain splashed up about nine or ten inches in no man's land, and it went on and on and on. That stopped the First Battle of Ypres, which was raging up north. Our sector north of Armentières ceased. The condition of the latrines can be imagined and we could not sleep, every minute was like an hour. The dead were lying out in front. The rains kept on, we were in yellow clay, and the water table was two feet below. Our trenches were seven feet deep. We walked about or moved very slowly in marl or pug or yellow watery clay. When the evening came and we could get out of it, it took about an hour to climb out. Some of our chaps slipped in and were drowned. They couldn't even be seen, but were trodden on later.

Some of our chaps slipped in and were drowned.

We were relieved after the fourth night and some of us had to be carried out. I noticed that many of the tough ones were carried out, while the skinny little whippersnappers like myself could somehow manage, we got out somehow as we had not the weight to carry. We marched back – slouched back – and eventually got to our billet at Plug Street (our nickname for Ploegsteert), a mile and a half away. We fell on the floor and slept, equipment on and everything. Everything was mud-slabbed – overcoats, boots and everything. We were dead beat. '

Lieutenant Charles Carrington
1/5th Battalion, Royal Warwickshire Regiment

'WHEN YOU CAME OUT OF THE LINE YOU WERE MENTALLY AND physically tired and hoped you were going to get a rest. But you didn't get much of a physical rest because almost every night you had to go on working parties up to the front line. The worst part was that for the last mile or two everything

LEFT: *A flooded dug-out in a front-line trench at Ploegsteert Wood, January 1917. In the grim conditions a sergeant of the Lancashire Fusiliers manages to smile.*

When you came out of the line you were mentally and physically tired and hoped you were going to get a rest.

had to be carried by hand – somehow or other you had to get up all the food, drinking water and necessary equipment.

This included rifle ammunition, machine-gun ammunition and trench-mortar ammunition, which was very clumsy, awkward stuff to handle. Then you had to carry enormous bundles of sandbags, balks of timber, planks, ready made-up duckboards and, worst of all, coils of barbed wire. Barbed wire is the most damnable stuff to handle. It was made up in coils that weighed half a hundredweight that we carried on a stick over two men's shoulders. You were very likely to cut your hands to ribbons before you got it there.

Private Clifford Lane
1st Battalion, Hertfordshire Regiment

FLEAS USED TO GET INTO THE seams of your underclothes, and the only way to get rid of them was to get a candle and go along the seams with the candle and you could hear the eggs crackling. And the extraordinary thing is these lice were so bad in places, I've seen men taking their shirts off with the skin of their backs absolutely raw where they'd been scratching. And there was no way of getting rid of them at all.

RIGHT: *Private Clifford Lane.*

Passing the Time

Much of the soldiers' time was spent waiting for action, but even at quiet times, life in the trenches was anxious and stressful. The enemy lines had to be watched twenty-four hours a day and there was the constant threat of unseen snipers, who might shoot at anyone whose head rose above ground level. Sudden attacks by enemy raiding parties were also a danger. Despite all this, life had to go on. The men still needed to eat, drink and rest and they were sometimes able to read books and write letters home while sitting in dugouts, tiny chambers hollowed out at the back of the trenches.

ABOVE: *Fixing scaling ladders the day before the Battle at Arras.*

Fleas used to get into the seams of your under-clothes and the only way to get rid of them was to use a candle.

Fusilier Victor Packer
Royal Irish Fusiliers

6I HAD HEARD ABOUT THE PREVIOUS BATTLES BUT I COULDN'T GET THERE fast enough. We had been brought up on the history of the Boer War and patriotism and heroics and everything, and we thought the war was going to be over before we could get there. However, in about half a minute all that had gone. I wondered what the devil I'd got into because it was nothing but mud and filth and all the chaps who were already there, well, they looked like tramps, all plastered with filth and dirt, and unshaven.

> *I wondered what the devil I'd got into because it was nothing but mud and filth and all the chaps who were already there, well, they looked like tramps. . .*

We couldn't dig trenches up there, because the ground was so soft and wet. We used to fill the sandbags and to get water we used to gouge out a hole at the side of the trench in the bottom of the wall of sandbags and put everything we could over it, a piece of cardboard or something or other, and in the morning that would be full of water, but it would be teeming with all little black things floating around, but we found that if we boiled it we killed all this stuff and could drink it quite well or brew it up for a drop of tea. Once we attempted to shave in it but it was cold water and it wasn't very clever because we couldn't light fires.

If you smoked you had to be very careful, if Jerry saw any smoke he would send a grenade over because he knew there was someone there, the same thing would give you away, but we got very clever at boiling a billy can, believe it or not, with love letters, letters from home. We would make spills of them and if you kept a constant flame under it you could make the water boil for tea, that was in the daytime. If it was at night, you had to cover it up with your coat or something. Then there were the rats, of course, rats. You would not kill rats because you had no means of getting rid of them, they would putrefy and it would be worse than if you left them alive. I think they lived in corpses, because they were huge, they were as big as cats, I am not exaggerating, some of them were as big as ordinary cats, horrible great things. **9**

Then there were the rats, of course, rats . . . they were as big as cats.

RIGHT: *Reconstruction of British troops moving into no-man's land in a wiring party on patrol.*

FIGHTING THE WAR

Many battles were fought on the Western Front, some of which were noted for the high numbers of casualties, the Battle of the Somme and the Second and Third Battles of Ypres among them. When the fighting was over there was often little land gained, but heavy human losses on both sides. Once the Western Front had been established at the end of 1914, the front line seldom moved.

BATTLE OF NEUVE CHAPELLE
10 – 13 March 1915

A surprise attack on the German trenches enabled British and Indian troops to capture the village of Neuve Chapelle in four hours, but their continued advance was halted on the third day. By then the element of surprise had been lost and the Germans had brought in reserves. Losses were high on both sides.

Sergeant Stefan Westmann
29th Division, German Army

'WHILE THE PRINCE REGENT OF BAVARIA LAUNCHED AN ATTACK ON Neuve Chapelle on January the 25th, this was only a feint to get the enemy to concentrate in the wrong area. Our attack was launched against the French and British trenches on the south of the Aire–La Bassée canal.

We got orders to storm the French position. We got in and I saw my comrades start falling to the right and left of me. But then I was confronted by a French corporal with his bayonet to the ready, just as I had mine. I felt the fear of death in that fraction of a second when I realised that he was after my life, exactly as I was after his. But I was quicker than he was, I pushed his rifle away and ran my bayonet through his chest. He fell, putting his hand on the place where I had hit him, and then I thrust again. Blood came out of his mouth and he died.

I nearly vomited. My knees were shaking and they asked me, 'What's the matter with you?' I remembered then that we had been told that a good soldier kills without thinking of his adversary as a human being – the very moment he sees him as fellow man, he's no longer a good soldier. My comrades were absolutely undisturbed by what had happened. One of them boasted that he had killed a *poilu* with the butt of his rifle. Another one had strangled a French captain. A third had hit somebody over the head with his spade. They were ordinary men like me. One was a tram conductor, another a commercial traveller, two were students, the rest farm workers – ordinary people who never would have thought to harm anybody.

But I had the dead French soldier in front of me, and how I would have liked him to have raised his hand! I would have shaken it and we would have been the best of friends because he was nothing but a poor boy – like me. A boy who had to fight with the cruellest weapons against a man who had nothing against him personally, who wore the uniform of another nation and spoke another language,

Why was it that we soldiers stabbed each other, strangled each other, went for each other like mad dogs?

but a man who had a father and mother and a family. So I woke up at night sometimes, drenched in sweat, because I saw the eyes of my fallen adversary. I tried to convince myself of what would've happened to me if I hadn't been quicker than him, if I hadn't thrust my bayonet into his belly first.

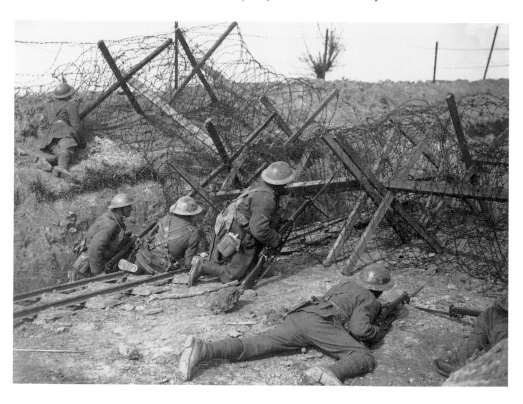

Why was it that we soldiers stabbed each other, strangled each other, went for each other like mad dogs? Why was it that we who had nothing against each other personally fought to the very death? We were civilised people after all, but I felt that the thin lacquer of civilisation of which both sides had so much, chipped off immediately. To fire at each other from a distance, to drop bombs, is something impersonal, but to see the whites of a man's eyes and then to run a bayonet into him – that was against my comprehension.

Corporal Alan Bray

WE TOOK UP POSITIONS NEAR KEMMEL HILL. IT WAS FOGGY AND THE attack was delayed two hours, which didn't do our spirits much good. Then the time came for us to go over. We had to run forward about fifty yards, up some planks over our own front-line trenches, and then across a meadow where it was almost impossible to run, we could only stagger along. As we were going over these planks about half of us were knocked out – either killed or wounded – and going across the meadow there were a lot more killed.

When we finally stopped and lay down, trying to get what shelter we could from the tremendous rifle fire which was coming over, a sergeant just in front of me jumped up and said, 'Come on men, be British.' So we jumped up again and followed him. He ran about six yards and then he went down too.

LEFT: *Battle of the Lys. Men of the 10th Battalion, Queen's Royal West Surrey Regiment, crouch behind a barbed wire defence.*

Well, then there were about a dozen of us left and we ran on another twenty yards towards the German trenches. Those trenches were literally packed – the men were standing four deep, firing machine guns and rifles straight at us, and the only shelter we could see was a road which ran up at right angles to the trench with a bank on the left-hand side. We managed to reach this bank but found ourselves looking straight up at the German trenches while they were firing straight down, gradually picking us off. Eventually there was only myself and another chap that weren't hit. **,**

SECOND BATTLE OF YPRES – THE HORROR OF GAS   22 April 1915

It was on this day that poison gas was first used in the war on the Western Front. Although the attack was made by the Germans, gas was used by both sides for the remainder of the war. At Ypres, however, Allied soldiers were taken completely by surprise by the mysterious yellow-green cloud that drifted over them. Without gas masks, they suffered terribly from the effects of the chlorine gas. Some died, others were ill for the rest of their lives. Gas masks were quickly rushed to the Front.

Various types of gases were used during the war. Some caused dreadful symptoms, making it impossible to breathe, or causing burns and blisters on the skin. They could blind a man for life. One type, called mustard gas, was virtually odourless but could stay in the ground for weeks and even penetrate a soldier's boots.

We just turned around and shot them as they were running away.

Private W. Underwood
1st Canadian Division

‘IT WAS A BEAUTIFUL DAY. I WAS LYING IN A FIELD WRITING A LETTER TO my mother, the sun was shining and I remember a lark singing high up in the sky. Then, suddenly, the bombardment started and we got orders to stand to.

We went up the line in two columns, one either side of the road. But as soon as we reached the outskirts of the village of St Julien the bullets opened up, and when I looked around I counted just thirty-two men left on their feet out of the whole company of 227. The rest of us managed to jump into ditches, and that saved us from being annihilated.

Then we saw coming towards us the French Zouaves. They were in blue coats and red pants and caps and it was a revelation to us, we hadn't seen anything but khaki and drab uniforms. They were rushing toward us, half staggering, and we wondered what was the matter. We were a little perturbed at first, then when they got to us we tried to rally them but they wouldn't stay. They were running away from the Germans. Then we got orders to shoot them down, which we did. We just turned around and shot them as they were running away.

ABOVE: *Argyll and Sutherland Highlanders wearing some of the first gas masks in May 1915.*

BELOW RIGHT: *Allied gas casualties in a field station in 1915.*

They were rushing toward us, half staggering, and we wondered what was the matter.

Then, as we looked further away, we saw this green cloud come slowly across the terrain. It was the first gas that anybody had seen or heard of, and one of our boys, evidently a chemist, passed the word along that this was chlorine. And he said, 'If you urinate on your handkerchiefs it will save your lungs, anyway.' So most of us did that, and we tied these handkerchiefs, plus pieces of putty or anything else we could find, around our faces, and it did save us from being gassed.

There were masses of Germans behind this gas cloud, we could see their grey uniforms as plain as anything, and there we were, helpless, with these Ross rifles that we couldn't fire because they were always jamming. '

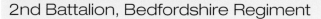
Private W. A. Quinton
2nd Battalion, Bedfordshire Regiment

‘The men came tumbling from the front line. I've never seen men so terror-stricken, they were tearing at their throats and their eyes were glaring out. Blood was streaming from those who were wounded and they were tumbling over one another. Those who fell couldn't get up because of the panic of the men following them, and eventually they were piled up two or three high in this trench. ’

I've never seen men so terror-stricken, they were tearing at their throats and their eyes were glaring out.

Lieutenant Victor Hawkins
2nd Battalion, Lancashire Fusiliers

'THE EFFECT OF THIS GAS WAS TO FORM A SORT OF FOAMY LIQUID IN one's lungs, which would more or less drown you. A lot of the men died pretty quickly, and others soon came down – they were in fact drowning from this beastly foam. Out of the 250 men we started with at 5 o'clock we were very soon down to about forty or fifty men. '

WHO WERE THE ALLIES?

The original Allied Powers were France, Russia and Great Britain (including her empire). They were joined throughout 1914 by Serbia, Montenegro, Belgium and Japan. In 1915 Italy joined them against Austria–Hungary (also against Germany in 1916). Romania and Portugal joined in 1916, followed by Greece in 1917. The United States declared war on 6 April 1917 and became an Associated Power. British dominions that took part in the war were Australia, Canada, New Zealand and South Africa. All British colonies sent troops or made an economic or manpower contribution to the Empire war effort. Soldiers from the British Empire in India fought, as did Unionist and Nationalist Irishmen.

Corporal Edward Glendinning
12th Battalion, Notts & Derby Reg (Sherwood Foresters)

'DURING THE NIGHT OF THE 24TH OF SEPTEMBER WE MOVED UP INTO reserve trenches almost opposite Hohenzollern Redoubt. As we came up we had passed through many squadrons of British cavalry who were assembling ready to exploit any breakthrough we infantrymen could make the next day. We didn't get any sleep all night, because even before we got there our artillery barrage was blazing away and we sat there huddling in this reserve communication trench.

Some chaps were crying, some praying, but most of us were optimistic.

BATTLE OF LOOS
25 September – 8 October 1915

The Battle of Loos was part of a larger campaign (the Artois–Loos Offensive) that was carried out by the French and British in autumn 1915. The Allies made their initial attack on 25 September but it was not successful. Hampered by supply problems and delays in getting reserves, it was finally called off. The Allies had greatly out-numbered the Germans, but ended up with many more casualties.

It was a long, dreary, miserable night. Some chaps were crying, some praying, but most of us were optimistic: we all hoped that we would come through.

As soon as it was light, we were issued with a big ration of rum. You could drink as much as you wanted. We were then told to be prepared to receive orders to advance at any moment. Any moment was a long while coming, which was very trying. It was two hours before we got the actual order to advance. Just before the order we were issued with two additional bandoliers of ammunition, which meant we were carrying a pretty heavy weight of ammunition.

We clambered out of the trench. Some of us had ladders and some got out as best they could. We very soon found ourselves picking our way over the bodies of men who had fallen in the earlier attack and wounded men who were trying to crawl into shell-holes to get protection. We kept on in extended order. For the first two or three hundred yards, there wasn't a great deal of firing. But all of a sudden they opened on us with terrific machine-gun fire, a lot of which came from a tall slag-heap on our right. I sensed we were getting fewer and fewer as we went on. From that time we received no further orders. We somehow took the second line of their trenches, which had been devastated by our artillery. We dug in and got ourselves into shallow trenches. Then the Germans began to realise where we were because they started sweeping us with machine-gun fire. Then they sent over shrapnel shells, but most of that burst behind us. Then they opened up with 'whizz-bangs'. We lost our platoon sergeant and corporal through direct hits. The hours wore on, it became dusk and we were relieved when a detachment of the Guards managed to take our places. They relieved us in much greater strength than we'd been all day. Whereas we'd been one man to ten yards of trench, they had a man every couple of feet. Word was passed along for the Sherwood Foresters to assemble in groups and to withdraw.

SHELLS

Huge numbers of shells were used in the First World War. A shell is an explosive device fired by a big gun and there were many different sizes and types: some exploded on impact, others were shrapnel shells designed to explode in flight to cause maximum damage and injury. Shells could also be filled with poison gas. Soldiers grew to recognise the sound that indicated the firing of an enemy shell and would run for cover. The term 'whizz-bang' was used to describe the sound a particular type of shell made.

ABOVE: *British attack on the Hohenzollern Redoubt, 13 October 1915.*

Some of them were still alive,

and they were crying out, begging for water

and plucking at our legs

as we went by.

Coming back over the ground that had been captured that day, the sight that met our eyes was quite unbelievable. If you can imagine a flock of sheep lying down sleeping in a field, the bodies were as thick as that. Some of them were still alive, and they were crying out, begging for water and plucking at our legs as we went by. One hefty chap grabbed me around both knees and held me. 'Water, water,' he cried. I was just going to take the cork out of my water-bottle – I had a little left – but I was immediately hustled on by the man behind me. 'Get on, get on, we are going to get lost in no man's land, come on.' So it was a case where compassion had to give way to discipline and I had to break away from this man to run up to catch up with the men in front. **'**

Lieutenant Ulrich Burke
2nd Battalion, Devonshire Regiment

' WHEN WE DID READ THE NEWSPAPERS IT MADE US ANGRY, ESPECIALLY IF you had done a big raid on a battalion scale which would be two hundred yards wide and you had penetrated the enemy to a depth of, we'll say, quarter or half a mile, brought back prisoners. Then you'd read in the paper 'No action on the Western Front'. It didn't seem to warrant, where you'd lost probably fifty men killed and an equal number wounded, a mention. It wasn't big enough, even though the war hadn't been on two years. It used to annoy everybody terribly, 'Very little action on the Western Front'. **'**

Fusilier W. Flynn
1st Battalion, Royal Munster Fusiliers

‘W HEN WE WOKE UP ON BOARD THE *RIVER CLYDE* IN THE MORNING AND looked out of the portholes and saw land, they told us it was the Dardanelles and we had to make a landing there. It was Cape Helles. We couldn't see anybody. All we could see was this piece of land shaped like a saucer which gradually went up to a little hill, which was called 141. That dominated the whole beach.

Our cue was when the Dublins came off the warship in cutters. We then had to run down the gangway across the two boats and a steam hopper, and then we only had perhaps ten or twenty feet to go to the shore.

But the boat had been carried away towards a strip of rock, and the steam hopper and one of the lighters had been cut away and drifted out to sea. The one that was tied to the bow of the ship was all right, but as we ran down the gangway, instead of having two separate gangways either side of the ship, they had connected them. Unfortunately, the first batch had to run across into the lighter, and what with us running down and them running across, and all the bodies piling up, it was like a barricade. They simply fell into the lighters. Some were dead, some were wounded, some weren't hit but got smothered in the pile-up.

Captain Geddes and I managed to get on the first lighter, where the dead were. Captain Geddes, said, 'It's no good Flynn, come on.' But I was weighed down by a big periscope I was carrying for him. We had double ammunition, double rations, double everything. He had the sense to tell everybody to throw their coats off before we made land. All the Dublins never had a chance to drop their coats, they went down, they sank – just disappeared.

All the Dublins never had a chance to drop their coats, they went down, they sank – just disappeared.

I followed Captain Geddes down the gangway and along the gunwale of the lighter, and we laid down in the bow with just enough cover to hide us. He looked back and called for the remainder of the company to come but they couldn't. So he said, 'Well, over we go, we're going to fall into the sea.' I managed to come up once or twice for fresh air, then gradually drifted to my right until I came up by

The Gallipoli landings

One of Germany's allies was the Ottoman Empire (Turkey). In early 1915 it was decided that the Allies would try to break through the Dardanelles Straits with the aim of capturing the Turkish capital, Constantinople. On 25 April troops from Britain, Australia, New Zealand, France and India landed on the Gallipoli peninsula. They were met with a tenacious Turkish defence.

Above: British troops in battle order, waiting to land on the Gallipoli Peninsula.

Eastern Front

— Front Line May 1915
— Front Line Dec 1916
— Furthest lines of Central Powers advance 1918

this strip of rock which was piled high with dead. Anyway, I managed just to crawl on the rock, exhausted.

We got along the side to the end of the boat without any mishap, there was about twelve feet of water to go through. The boat was facing ashore. So I dived into the water and crawled along the bottom and eventually came up behind the boat. It just hid us. Although when the waves wobbled a bit it turned the boat's stern into the shore and the enemy could just see us. We didn't realise this until I heard something go by and I said to Captain Geddes, 'My, that was close,' and he said, 'It was, wasn't it.'

It was then that his ear was shot off and I don't know how it missed me, but it did. He said, 'We'd better get ashore, but how can we?' I said, 'We'll have to go underneath, if there's enough room. Wait till the waves lift the boat and shove your rifle in front of you.' Anyway, we managed to scramble on the shore with eight or nine feet to go, and we got behind a bank about five feet high, where we were safe for the time being.

Private Walter Stagles
3rd Australian Battalion

'ON THE MORNING WHEN THE ATTACK CAME, THEY CAME OVER IN TWO great waves from their trenches, in great hulking mass. They were rather big men, the Turks, fine body of men. As they came over, they were shouting 'Allah!' and blowing their trumpets and whistling and shouting, like schoolboys. As they got closer, within nice rifle range, we had the order to fire and we opened up with rapid fire and brought them down in hundreds, hundreds of them fell, and in front of our trenches. I should think when the attack was over there would be anything from two to three thousand dead or dying in front of our brigade.

SECOND BATTLE OF KRITHIA
6 – 8 May 1915

This was the second attempt by the Allies to break through the Turkish lines and capture the village of Krithia. After the first failed attack, this battle was rather more successful and Allied soldiers managed to push the Turkish line back by almost a kilometre. However, losses were high and their strategic aim of capturing Achi Baba was not carried out. A further attempt was made in June.

Ordinary Seaman Joe Murray
Hood Battalion, Royal Naval Division

'I REMEMBER, YATES WAS A LITTLE AHEAD OF DON TOWNSEND AND myself. We crawled up more or less abreast, but the bullets were hitting the sand, spraying us, hitting our packs. So we decided, 'How about another dash?' So off we went, near enough fifteen yards. Then we got down again. Then we decided to go a little bit further. We'd got to keep bearing to our right slightly, because we were dodging the line of fire. We decided to go a little bit further and all four of us got up together.

Yates was in front and all of a sudden he bent over. He'd been shot in the stomach, or maybe the testicles, and he danced around like a cat on hot bricks until he fell down on the ground. We decided to ease up a bit. But as soon as we got near him he got up and rushed like hell at the Turks and Bang! He went down altogether, out for the count.

> *Poor Horton, he kept crying for his mother. I can see him now. Hear him at this very moment.*

Horton and I were more or less together. Townsend was on the other side and there was a gap where Yates had been. Young Horton was the first to get to Yates and he had just pushed him to see what was wrong when a bullet struck him dead centre of the brow – it went right through his head and took out a bit of my knuckle. Poor Horton, he kept crying for his mother. I can see him now. Hear him at this very moment. He said he was eighteen but I don't think he was sixteen, never mind eighteen. He was such a frail young laddie. He was a steward on the Fyffe banana boats in peacetime. Yates was dead. Horton was dead. Only Don and I were left. **'**

RIGHT: *Men of the King's Own Scottish Borderers go over the top in the battle of Krithia on 4 June.*

Private Harold Boughton
2/1st Battalion, London Regiment

❝ONE OF THE BIGGEST CURSES WAS FLIES. MILLIONS AND MILLIONS OF flies. The whole of the side of the trench used to be one black swarming mass. Anything you opened, like a tin of bully, would be swarming with flies. If you were lucky enough to have a tin of jam and opened that, swarms of flies went straight into it. They were all around your mouth and on any cuts or sores that you'd got, which then turned septic. Immediately you bared any part of your body you were smothered. It was a curse, it really was. ❞

Ordinary Seaman Jack Gearing
Benbow Battalion, Royal Naval Division

'EACH DAY WHEN THERE WAS A LULL WE'D GO IN AND COLLECT THE wounded. Some of them were terribly badly wounded, and all so young. Suvla Bay was reasonably flat and the soldiers had made homes for themselves or taken over where other battalions had been before they moved forward. I did my best to cheer them up and encourage them. But most of the time, I was quiet because there wasn't much you could say in the face of all that horror. It was important that they had their own thoughts, they had to come to terms with it in their own way.

Every Sunday we used to try and have a service on board and we sang hymns which were heard by the soldiers on shore. They told us how much it meant to

them so whenever we scrubbed the decks we sang out as loud as we could all the old hymns to inspire them: 'Onward, Christian Soldiers', 'Fight the Good Fight', anything that was rousing. It cheered us up, too. **'**

Fusilier W. Flynn
1st Battalion, Royal Munster Fusiliers

' WE DID GET BLACK TOWARDS THE END. We weren't succeeding at all, all we were doing was losing a lot of men and ships. Every day we were bringing in different men, different faces, all tired, all beaten. And it was so hot that summer, so hot. Then, as autumn came on, we knew things were getting worse on land, even with the reinforcements. We were watching a picture of failure fought out by brave men.

LEAVING GALLIPOLI

The Gallipoli campaign was not a success for Allied troops. They suffered heavy losses and withdrew in January 1916. Not a single man was lost during the evacuation.

When we withdrew on the 20th of December it was dark. The soldiers were all packed so tight and quiet in the barges making their way to the big ships. We never lost a man, which was remarkable. As we were steaming quietly away I thought of what 'Pincher' Martin, who had done twenty years in the Navy, had said to me a few days after we'd arrived at Suvla Bay: 'We're not going to be flying the Union Jack here.' He was right. We were never going to make it ours. **'**

LEFT: *Australian soldiers who took the brunt of casualties attend a wounded friend. None of them have steel helmets as these were not issued until 1916.*

We weren't succeeding at all, all we were doing was losing a lot of men and ships.

BATTLE OF THE SOMME
1 July – 18 November 1916

In February 1916 the Germans mounted an attack on the French at Verdun. The town was held, but the resulting siege lasted many months and the French were not sure how much longer they could hold on. To take the pressure off them, Allied commanders planned an attack on the Germans north and south of the River Somme. In June they bombarded the Germans for seven days, using a vast number of shells, before they mounted the infantry attack on 1 July.

Lieutenant Stefan Westmann
German Medical Officer

❛For a full week we were under incessant bombardment. Day and night, the shells came upon us. Our dugouts crumbled. They would fall on top of us and we'd have to dig ourselves and our comrades out. Sometimes we'd find them suffocated or smashed to pulp. Soldiers in the bunkers became hysterical – they wanted to run out, and fights developed to keep them in the comparative safety of our deep bunkers. Even the rats became hysterical and came into our flimsy shelters to seek refuge from this terrific artillery fire.

For seven days and seven nights we had nothing to eat and nothing to drink while shell after shell burst upon us. ❜

Lieutenant Colonel Alfred Irwin
8th Battalion, East Surrey Regiment

❛We had a lot of warning that the battle of the Somme was coming. It was such a big show, and the first of its kind. I'm quite certain the Boche knew as much about it as we did. He knew when we were coming, and if he hadn't the barrage would have told him, as for the two or three days before the Somme it

'GOING OVER THE TOP'

ABOVE: *Troops advancing during the Battle of the Somme, 1916.*

When a large-scale attack on the enemy was planned, such as that at the Somme, the procedure was to first weaken their defence by bombardment with artillery. Heavy artillery was brought up by horse and tractor to the Front and used to bring down a devastating barrage of fire on the opposing line. The infantry, armed with rifles and bayonets, would then follow the barrage up by moving forward out of their trenches to advance on the enemy line. The moment of emerging from the trench to face the enemy was called 'going over the top'.

Following the massive bombardment the soldiers who went over the top on 1 July expected to advance towards the Germans relatively easily. They were unaware that the German barbed wire hadn't been destroyed and that many of their soldiers were taking shelter in concrete bunkers. The British infantry had little chance and many were quickly mown down by enemy machine-gun fire. It was a disaster and the worst day ever for the British Army. On that first day alone, there were nearly 20,000 British soldiers killed and 40,000 wounded.

was intensive, in order to break up the wire in front of the front line.

We were all very young and optimistic, and for myself, I didn't think much about the future. I took it for granted that the wire would be cut, that we'd massacre the Boche in their front line, get to our objective and then be sent to do something else next day.

We were all very young and optimistic, and for myself, I didn't think much about the future.

I was battalion commander on the first day and it was difficult to know exactly what to do. One's instinct was to get on with the chaps, and to see what was going on. On the other hand, we'd been warned over and over again that officers' lives must not be thrown away in doing something they

ABOVE: On the first day of the Somme, the British blew up a mine containing 27.5 tonnes of explosive, which created a massive crater near La Boisselle.

oughtn't – in fact that commanding officers should lead from behind, and only go forward when the attack had lost its impetus. And that's what I tried to do.

Captain Nevill was commanding B Company, and a few days before the battle he came to me with a suggestion. He said that as he and his men were all equally ignorant of what their conduct would be when they got into action, he thought it might be helpful – as he had 400 yards to go and he knew it would be covered by machine-gun fire – if he could furnish each platoon with a football and allow them to kick it forward and follow it.

I sanctioned the idea on condition that he and his officers really kept command of their units and didn't allow it to develop into a rush after the ball. If a man came across the football, he could kick it forward but he mustn't chase after it. I think myself, it did help them enormously, it took their minds off it. **,**

Lieutenant Stefan Westmann
German Medical Officer

'Then the British Army went over the top. The very moment we felt their artillery fire was directed against the reserve positions, our machine-gunners crawled out of the bunkers, red-eyed and dirty, covered in the blood of their fallen comrades, and opened up a terrific fire.'

Captain Alfred Irwin
8th Battalion, East Surrey Regiment

'They went forward shouting with such energy, kicking the football ahead of them. But so quickly Neville and his second in command were both killed, plus his company sergeant-major. I picked up all the chaps I could and went over the parapet by myself. I stood well out in the open and said, 'Come on, come on, come on,' and they all came on quite smoothly.

Eventually we reached the German third reserve line. We were so lamentably few that there was very little we could do that night, so I posted the men as well as I could and while we were heavily shelled we weren't attacked, and the next day we were relieved. We'd come down from eight hundred men to something under two hundred in that attack, and it seemed to me a dreadful waste of life.

All my best chaps had gone. We buried eight young officers in one grave before we left. It was a terrible massacre. I think the attack should have been called off until the wire had been cut. I think they ought to have known what the condition of the wire was through their intelligence officers before we ever got to July the 1st.'

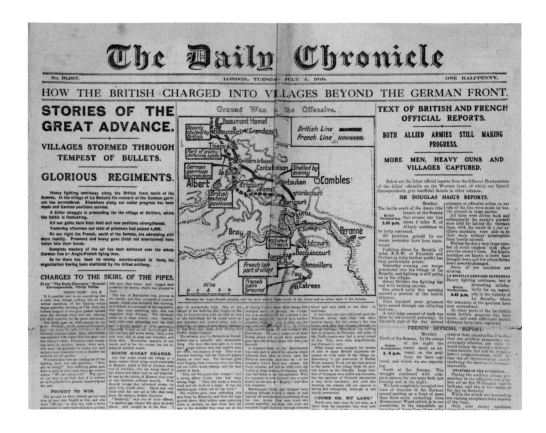

The Daily Chronicle

No. 16,967.   LONDON, TUESDAY, JULY 4, 1916.   ONE HALFPENNY.

HOW THE BRITISH CHARGED INTO VILLAGES BEYOND THE GERMAN FRONT.

STORIES OF THE GREAT ADVANCE.

VILLAGES STORMED THROUGH TEMPEST OF BULLETS.

GLORIOUS REGIMENTS.

CHARGES TO THE SKIRL OF THE PIPES.

TEXT OF BRITISH AND FRENCH OFFICIAL REPORTS.

BOTH ALLIED ARMIES STILL MAKING PROGRESS.

MORE MEN, HEAVY GUNS AND VILLAGES CAPTURED.

SIR DOUGLAS HAIG'S REPORTS.

FRENCH OFFICIAL REPORT.

Lieutenant Montague Cleeve
Royal Garrison Artillery

"ONE THING I SHALL NEVER FORGET WAS MY FIRST EXPERIENCE OF DEAD bodies. On the first day at Albert the weather was very hot, and I was sent up to an observation post. I went with a marvellous officer who was later killed, a splendid young subaltern called Priddy. We found we literally couldn't walk along the trenches without treading on dead bodies, German and British. The stench and the flies were simply appalling. That was one of the most miserable memories I have of the Somme. It was pathetic really. Eventually one just got over it and thought nothing of it. We couldn't help it, we were alive and that's what mattered. And being alive, we jolly well had to get on with it."

'All the world's dead – they're all dead – they're all dead.' That's all I could think as I crawled along.

Private Charles Taylor
13th Battalion, Yorks and Lancs

❝ I STARTED CRAWLING TOWARDS OUR LINES, AND I HAD NEVER SEEN SO many dead men clumped together. That was all I could see and I thought to myself, 'All the world's dead – they're all dead – they're all dead.' That's all I could think as I crawled along. Everywhere I passed, to my left and right were dead men laying on the ground. ❞

Captain Herbert Sulzbach
German Artillery

❝ ONE SUMMER EVENING SOON AFTER THE BATTLE OF THE SOMME HAD started, the guns were rumbling and there was a terrible noise of battle in our ears. Yet where we lay, just thirty metres from the trenches, there were mountains and peace, and hardly any shooting. We could see the French soldiers, and one night a Frenchman started to sing – he was a wonderful tenor. None of us dared to shoot and suddenly we were all looking out from the trenches and applauding, and the Frenchman said 'Merci'. It was peace in the middle of war, and the strange thing was that just a few kilometres northwards the terrible battle of the Somme was going on. ❞

Lieutenant Montague Cleeve
Royal Garrison Artillery

IT WAS A COMPLETE AND UTTER SURPRISE TO THE GERMANS THAT WE HAD ever devised such a thing as a tank. They were so shattered when they first appeared on the Somme that all resistance in the German section where they were used collapsed. The mistake we made then was not to have prepared for this lack of opposition. We should have had our cavalry all ready to take over from the tanks and wipe the whole thing out. We could have turned the flank of the Germans in no time. But the success of the tanks took us by surprise and we were so ill-prepared that nobody followed them up.

THE FIRST TANKS

It was on the Somme that tanks were used in warfare for the first time. These heavy-duty vehicles were specifically constructed by the British to break through the German trenches, but the Mark I tank had varying degrees of success. Some failed mechanically but more ground was gained with the tanks than at any other time during the battle. Later in the war, more reliable tanks played a significant part in the Battle of Cambrai and during the Allies' advance in 1918.

ABOVE: *The Mark I tank used at the Battle of the Somme, much to the astonishment of the enemy.*

The German resistance collapsed until they began shooting at the tanks when they were miles ahead of the former British front line. Then they had to come limping back, one by one, and that was an end to the thing.

The tanks had a complete walk-through. I remember seeing one moving at Pozières, it just crawled on and on – bumping into shell-holes, nose up, then climbing out, then diving down into another, then diving up again and not quite making it. That gave the Germans the opportunity they needed to direct their machine guns at it, and it soon became a complete wreck by everybody shooting at it.

I don't know what happened to that crew, but the tanks represented a missed opportunity. Had we only followed them up with cavalry, or any mobile troops, we could have got fifteen miles or so behind the German lines under their protection, then captured the German headquarters and turned the whole result of the Somme. ,

Corporal Clifford Lane
1st Battalion, Hertfordshire Regiment

'THE WINTER OF 1916 WAS SO COLD I FELT LIKE CRYING. I'D NEVER FELT like it before, not even under shellfire. What I had felt under shellfire, especially during the first two years, was a wish for a wound, a 'Blighty wound' we called them, to get me home. You thought a 'Blighty wound' was the most fortunate thing that could happen to you.

But there were times, after being shelled for hours on end during the latter part of the Somme battle, that all I wanted was to be blown to bits. Because you knew that if you got wounded, they could never get you away, not under those conditions. You'd see other people with internal wounds and you thought your only hope was to get killed outright, your only relief. It wasn't only me who felt like that, it happened to lots of people.

Major Richard Talbot Kelly
Royal Artillery

IT RAINED ABSOLUTELY CONTINUOUSLY, ONE WAS AS AFRAID OF GETTING drowned as of getting hit by shells. Actually the extraordinary quagmire nature of the Passchendaele battle masked much of the effect of the shells, which sank so deeply into the mud that the splinter and blast effect was to a large extent nullified. But half the men in my battery were suffering from ague. I had only one sergeant left on his feet and I was the only officer left at the guns. But it was the weather, more than anything else, that got one down. When one woke in the morning in the little scrape you'd scratched out of the ground to get out of the way of the worst of the splinters, you felt the water bubbling and oozing in the small of your back.

It rained absolutely continuously, one was as afraid of getting drowned as of getting hit by shells.

THIRD BATTLE OF YPRES (PASSCHENDAELE)
31 July – 10 November 1917

British troops were ordered to carry out a major assault that started off with a ten-day bombardment. Despite this, the Germans held off the Allied advance, though some small gains were made on the left flank. The bombardment itself, combined with heavy rainfall, turned the ground to swamp and conditions were almost impossible for fighting. Men and horses were drowning in mud. The first attack was eventually called off but fighting resumed in late September when British forces managed to capture the ridge east of Ypres. Three more attacks took place in October and on 6 November the village of Passchendaele was finally taken by Canadian troops. Once again, there were a large number of casualties.

LEFT: *In the deep mud of Passchendaele in 1917 soldiers try and dig out an 18-pounder gun.*

Lieutenant Ulrich Burke
2nd Battalion, Devonshire Regiment

‘WHEN YOU GET OUT ON TOP YOU TRY AND KEEP IN AS STRAIGHT A LINE as possible. You're spaced at three- to four-yard intervals and you go forward at the high port, that is, with the rifle diagonally across your chest and the bayonet pointing upwards towards the sky.

We reckoned to do a hundred yards in a minute to a minute and a half. I know one can run it in ten seconds. But with the men having to go round the shell-holes, and at the same time being fired on and trying to keep their distance between one another and keep their alignment, it was only when you got to within twenty yards of the trench that you said, 'Charge!' They then brought their rifles down, charged into the trench and killed and bayoneted the enemy.

We then headed for Lake Farm. There our commanding officer was killed. The second in command took over and we went on a bit further. When we got to the enemy trench we jumped in. This German put his bayonet up and I caught it in the right shoulder, right across my back. It just missed my spine but I was impaled on it. My great fear was that he would press the trigger, which would have made a hell of a mess. But my sergeant, who was nearby, saw this, came in close, shot the fellow and then hoisted me off the bayonet with the help of another man. I was on top of this dead German and it wasn't pleasant. A bayonet wound hurts directly it goes in and the withdrawal is even more anguished than the putting in, because at least the putting in is instantaneous. If you get hit by a bullet or bomb splinter it's so hot that it cauterises the wound and you don't feel anything for a minute or so. '

Lieutenant Hartwig Pohlmann
36th Prussian Division

' On SEPTEMBER THE 20TH THE GREAT ATTACK OF THE HIGHLAND Division met our own regiment. The firing went on for several hours, even after the Highlanders had stormed our front line and were trying to get onwards through all these shell-holes. We sprang from shell-hole to shell-hole. The fire was so heavy I didn't notice the single shells. We advanced and drove the Highlanders back a bit, but we couldn't reach the front line where our third battalion had been vanquished. They were all gone, some dead, some taken prisoner, we didn't see any of them again. We happened to catch some of the Highlanders, and it was a funny sight for us to see soldiers with kilts and naked knees. **"**

LEFT: *Lieutenant Ulrich Burke.*

RIGHT: *A padre giving comfort to a wounded man from the Battle of Menin Road Ridge (20–25 September 1917).*

Private Harry Patch
Duke of Cornwall's Light Infantry

" At PILCKEM RIDGE I CAN STILL SEE THE BEWILDERMENT AND FEAR ON THE men's faces when we went over the top. C and D Company was support, A and B had had to go at the front line. All over the battlefield the wounded were lying down, English and German all asking for help. We weren't like the Good Samaritan in the Bible, we were the robbers who passed by and left them. You couldn't help them. I came across a Cornishman, ripped from shoulder to waist with shrapnel, his stomach on the ground beside him in a pool of blood. As I got to him he said, 'Shoot me.' He was beyond all human aid. Before we could even draw a revolver he had died. He just said 'Mother.' I will never forget it. **"**

Lieutenant Charles Carrington
1/5th Battalion, Royal Warwickshire Regiment

'THE NOISE WOULD GROW INTO A GREAT CRESCENDO AND AT A CERTAIN point your nerve would break. In a flash of time, in a fifth of a second, you'd decide that this was the one. You'd throw yourself down into the mud and cringe at the bottom of the shell-hole. All the other people around would be doing the same.

Sometimes you miscalculated and this wasn't a shell for you, and it would go sailing busily on and plonk down on somebody else four hundred yards away. When a shell arrived it would drop into the mud and burst with a shattering shock. The killing splinters flew off and might fly fifty yards away from the point of impact. You could find a fragment of red-hot jagged iron weighing half a pound arriving in your shell-hole.

You'd throw yourself down into the mud and cringe at the bottom of the shell-hole.

They'd take another second or two before they would all settle down in the mud. Then you'd get up and roar with laughter, and the others would laugh at you for having been the first one to throw yourself down. This of course was hysterics! It becomes a kind of game in which you cling on and try not to let the tension break. The first person in a group who shows a sign of fear by giving way and taking cover – he'd lose a point and it counted against him. The one who held out longest had gained a point – but in what game? What was this for?

After eighteen months in France I was still trying to pretend to be brave and not succeeding very well, and so were we all. All the time one was saying to oneself, 'If they can take it – I can take it!', the awful thing being that this was not an isolated experience but one which went on continuously, minute after minute and even hour after hour. **'**

Bombardier J. W. Palmer
26th Brigade, Royal Field Artillery

'IT WAS MUD, MUD, EVERYWHERE: MUD IN THE TRENCHES, MUD IN FRONT of the trenches, mud behind the trenches. Every shell-hole was a sea of filthy oozing mud. I suppose there's a limit to everything, but the mud of Passchendaele – to see men sinking into the slime, dying in the slime – I think it absolutely finished me off.

I knew, for the three months before I was wounded, that I was going to get it. The only thing was, I thought I was going to get killed. Every time I went out to mend the wire I think I was the biggest coward on God's earth. Nobody knew when a wire would go, but we knew that it had to be mended, the infantrymen's lives depended on those wires working. It didn't matter whether or not we'd had any sleep, we just had to keep those wires going.

Every shell-hole was a sea of filthy oozing mud.

There were many days when I simply don't know what happened because I was so damned tired. The fatigue in that mud was something terrible. You reached a point where there was no beyond, you just couldn't go any further. The night I reached my lowest ebb I'd been out on the wire all day and all night, I hadn't had any rest, it seemed, for weeks. It was very, very difficult to mend a telephone wire in this mud. You'd find one end and then you'd try and trudge through the mud to find the other end, but as you got one foot out the other one would sink down again.

It was somewhere near midnight. The Germans were sending over quite a barrage and I crouched down in one of these dirty shell-holes. I began to think of those poor devils who'd been punished for self-inflicted wounds – some had even been shot. I began to wonder if I could get out of it. I sat there and kept thinking, it's very lonely when you're on your own. Then in the distance I heard the rattle of a harness. I knew there were ammunition wagons coming up and I thought, 'Well, here's a way out – when they get level with me I'll ease out and put my leg under the wheel and I can plead it was an accident.'

It was very, very difficult to mend a telephone wire in this mud.

I waited as the sound of the harness got nearer and nearer. Eventually I saw the leading horses' heads in front of me and I thought, 'This is it!' and began to ease my way out as the first wagon reached me. But you know, I never even had the guts to do it, I just couldn't do it. I think I was broken in spirit and mind.

ABOVE: *Wiring party carrying reels of telephone cable along narrow duckboards towards Pilckem.*

Sergeant-Major Richard Tobin
Hood Battalion, Royal Naval Division

'THERE WAS NO CHANCE OF BEING WOUNDED AND GETTING A 'BLIGHTY ONE' at Passchendaele. You could either get through or die, because if you were wounded and slipped off the duckboards you just sank into the mud. I don't know how far the duckboards extended because it was such slow going up to the Front, but there were hundreds and hundreds of yards zigzagging about. At each side was a sea of mud, and if you stumbled you would go in up to the waist, and literally every pool was full of the decomposed bodies of humans and mules.'

ANIMALS IN THE WAR

In 1917, one million animals were serving with British forces. Pigeons and dogs helped carry out the important job of delivering messages. Horses pulled ambulance carts and ammunition wagons though the best horses were allotted to the cavalry. Both horses and mules were used to pull artillery to the front lines and to carry supplies. Finding enough food for the animals, who often bore heavy loads, was a constant problem.

ABOVE: *German cavalry on the move in June 1918. Both soldiers and horses are equipped to deal with a gas attack.*

Private Raynor Taylor
Welch Regiment

‘THE BATTALION HALTED ALONG THE ROADSIDE FOR THE USUAL TEN minutes. Suddenly we were called upon to stand up because the King was coming along this road and we were expected to cheer him. This cavalcade came along, the King in his car, and the officers did cheer but I've no recollection of any of the men cheering. After a period in the front line, you weren't in any mood to cheer anybody. ’

Captain Douglas Wimberley
232nd Machine Gun Company, Machine Gun Corps

'THE WIRE AT CAMBRAI WAS ABOUT FOUR FOOT HIGH AND FIFTEEN YARDS wide, but the tanks that had gone in front of us had ploughed through it like a ship in the sea, and we had no difficulty at all in following their tracks. We also got over the Hindenburg front line. That was an enormous trench, about eight feet deep and fifteen feet wide, but again we were able to get over quite easily.

Getting our mules over wasn't so easy, but luckily there were quite a lot of Germans there who were more or less looking for someone to surrender to, so they helped us get them across.

> **BATTLE OF CAMBRAI**
> 20 November – 3 December 1917
>
> The British made mass use of their tanks for the first time and were initially successful, forcing the Germans back six kilometres and breaking through the German trench systems of the Hindenburg Line. Many German prisoners were taken. However, a successful German counter-attack later in the month retook all that had been gained by the British.

When it became really light it was a wonderful sight.

When it became really light it was a wonderful sight. We could see the lines of tanks ahead of us going down the slope towards the Grand Ravine and the lines of Jocks slowly moving along behind them. As we passed, there were numbers of Germans in every direction. The ones near us were really just trying to surrender, but further down the slopes we could see quite a lot more running around trying to escape from the tanks.

They'd left their trenches and dugouts – probably rightly – because had they stayed they'd have got Mills bombs from the Jocks. They were a very poor type of German – they were small, unshaven and dirty, and quite a lot were wearing spectacles, rather like the cartoons of the time of what the Germans were supposed to look like.

ABOVE: *Men of the 11th Battalion, Leicestershire Regiment, with machine guns in a captured second line trench during the Battle of Cambrai, November 1917.*

Later on we got into position and began shooting 'overhead fire', over the lines of the advancing Jocks. The extraordinary thing was that for about three minutes I had to stop firing altogether, as a great number of Boche came straight towards our machine guns with their hands up, and it would have been absolute sheer massacre to have killed them. **,**

Lieutenant Miles Reinke
2nd Guards Dragoons, German Army

WHEN THE FIRST TANKS PASSED THE FIRST LINE, WE THOUGHT WE WOULD be compelled to retreat towards Berlin. I remember one tank, by the name of Hyena, which advanced very far then suddenly stopped about a thousand yards

THE HINDENBURG LINE

In September 1916 the Germans began to build a vast system of trenches and concrete defences across northern France. This was known as the 'Hindenburg Line' and it was the last and the strongest of their defences on the Western Front. The Allies did not break through until October 1918.

ABOVE: *British cavalry crossing a wooden bridge over the River Somme at Brie, near Péronne, March 1917.*

from my little dugout. Some of the boys soon discovered they could stop the tanks by throwing a hand grenade into the manhole on the top. Once this was known, the boys realised that there was a blind spot – that the machine guns couldn't reach every point around the tank, and these points were very important in the defence.

I was shocked and felt very sorry for those fellows in the tanks, because there was no escape for them. Once a man was on top of the tank it was doomed to failure, and the poor fellows were not able to escape. The fuel would start to burn and after an hour and a half or two hours we saw only burning tanks in front and behind us. Then the approaching infantry behind the tanks still had to overcome the machine guns of our infantry. These were still effective because the British artillery had to stop shooting as the tanks were advancing, and naturally some of our machine-gun nests were still in full action.

Anyhow, the attack came to a standstill and we waited for several regiments of cavalry to sweep up and drive us towards Berlin. But this didn't happen, much to our surprise. When new troops were pulled together near this break-in of the British tanks, the situation settled down, we were formed anew, and afterwards we could clearly see the spot where the British tanks had driven into the German lines. Then after a few days we made a counter-attack. It didn't succeed on the first or the second day, but on the third day we were finally successful.

Once a man was on top of the tank it was doomed to failure, and the poor fellows were not able to escape.

Major Hartwig Pohlmann
36th Prussian Division

ON THE 19TH OF MARCH WE GOT OUR ORDERS TO GO INTO THE preparation positions. During the night, behind the front line, there was a lot of traffic carrying ammunition and bringing into position the guns. There was very much life and a lot of people moving in the trenches. On the 20th we got the

THE GERMAN BREAKTHROUGH, 21 MARCH 1918

Aided by large numbers of troops brought back from the Eastern Front, as a result of Russia leaving the war, the German army broke through Allied lines and pushed them back beyond all their previous gains. The Somme was overrun in four days. Thousands of Allied soldiers surrendered. The Germans continued to advance and by June were back on the River Marne.

order, tomorrow morning the attack will start – we got a high feeling. We were in high spirits because we hoped for our victory in this battle. That night about 3 am I got out of my dugout to look round. The night was silent, nothing was to be heard, and there was a clear sky, stars shining and glittering. I thought these are the same stars that my family at home will look at.

At 9 am I stood up and had a little breakfast and then left my dugout. I could see nothing. It was thick fog. I thought how can we attack in this? Nevertheless we had to attack. I told my soldiers to hang on with one hand to the belt of the man in front, but they couldn't do that for long because the ground was very rough and we had to creep through barbed wire. So soon there was a pell-mell, but everyone knew that they had to go straight on. The soldiers that lost their own companies made contact with other companies and followed them. Soon I had soldiers of several companies of my regiment together and they followed me. As we advanced through the fog we suddenly heard guns firing behind us. We realised that we had come out behind a British battery which was firing barrage fire. They didn't know that we had broken through. One of my men laid a hand on the shoulder of the British officer and said: 'Cease fire.' They were stunned. **,**

BELOW: *Two British soldiers killed during the German advance of 21 March 1918. Someone has taken their boots.*

Corporal Sidney Amatt
7th Battalion, Essex Regiment

'WE WERE GIVEN INSTRUCTIONS TO RETIRE. AS WE LOOKED OVER WE SAW that the Germans had advanced on our left flank and on our right and they were behind us only a hundred yards away. Somehow we arrived at what had been a reserve trench. There a sergeant of the Machine Gun Corps told us to go down the dugout out of the way of the shellfire. We all bundled down this dugout and when we got down there we saw an officer who said: 'Next time you're relieved, you'll be relieved by the Germans,' and he made some coffee for us. We had left one man as a sentry at the top of the dugout. Suddenly he yelled down to us that the Germans were in the trench. As we made ready to go up the steps, he came down and joined us. I expect he was terrified.

Next thing, we heard a German voice up above. One of the chaps with us who knew a little German said he's calling down that we've got to surrender. Anyway, the next thing we heard was a grenade bouncing down the steps – it was a rather terrifying experience – as we knew it was going to explode at the bottom. There was nowhere for us to go. We cowered there. It exploded and a corporal close to it was splattered with a lot of small pieces of this grenade but everyone else was all right. We were ordered to come up with our hands up. When we got to the top he said we were ordered to say 'Kamerad', which we did because there was a big unter-officer – like our sergeant-major – with a Luger pistol which he pressed into your ribs and looked at you with a mean look. If you said 'Kamerad', he'd

When we got to the top of the trench I was astonished to find that the whole area we'd occupied a few hours before was swarming with Germans.

nod you on and you went up the trench and were all collected together. When we got to the top of the trench I was astonished to find that the whole area we'd occupied a few hours before was swarming with Germans. The whole army was moving forward.

THE AMERICAN IMPACT

In April 1917 the United States entered the war and American troops began to cross the Atlantic. By the summer of 1918 American soldiers were arriving in France at the rate of 300,000 a month. Most of them were inexperienced but their health, stamina and enthusiasm boosted the morale of the much-weakened Allied troops. Their numbers soon began to have an impact on the outcome of the war.

Sergeant Melvin Krulewitch
United States Marine Corps

WE LEFT NEW YORK AND SAILED IN A CONVOY OF SEVEN OR EIGHT ships, including some very important warships. We were, of course, under twenty-four-hour alert; we had submarine warnings about halfway across, and several submarine attacks during the trip. As we neared the French coast and the coast of Ireland – in that general line from Ireland to France – we were met by a group of camouflaged destroyers. It was a most welcome sight, because we were in a danger zone, and they would flit in and out between the ships, giving us an assurance of safety.

We came through all right, with no losses, and landed at Brest. On the trip across we'd had to impose many restrictions: sleeping quarters were tight and we all slept in hammocks; and we had an allowance of just a small amount of water each. That water was used for brushing the teeth, then washing the face, then for washing your hands and finally for washing your clothes – all in the same bucket.

We had submarine attack exercises every day, when some men went to the gun crews and others to the boats in order to prepare us for an emergency, should it come about. Some of the men hadn't had any experience of sailing abroad and they were a little – shall we say – queasy at times. But by and large the crossing was a tremendous success, and all the men in my platoon were well trained and active, and ready and eager to get into the battle itself.

We learned trench practice and how to handle ourselves in night raids and night marches.

When we got to France there was intensive training from French and British instructors, who had already had three years' experience of the war and could give us the benefit of that right at the start. We learned trench practice and how to handle ourselves in night raids and night marches. We learned how to handle a knife, which we hadn't learned before, although all of us carried a dirk. We also learned the raider attack, which was common in trench warfare, because both sides would occasionally make a night raid to a part of the enemy line to get a prisoner, or some information or documents.

So we were trained right down to the bone. These men were like eagles newly washed, which I think is what Churchill called the British soldiers landing at the Dardanelles. And our boys were ready for war; we awaited the call; we were no jingoes, we were no screamers around for this or that, but we were regular marines and we were trained for war – that was our profession. **'**

Corporal Clifford Lane
1st Battalion, Hertfordshire Regiment

'I THINK IF THE AMERICANS HADN'T COME IN it would have been stalemate, in which case – because the Germans had had enough, too – there would have been a negotiated peace. But the fact was that suddenly there were all these Americans, hundreds of thousands of strong, healthy, well-equipped lads

whose strength hadn't been impaired in any way. They were ready to go – just as we had been in 1914. So you can just imagine what the Germans thought, they knew what was going to happen. That was why they were so desperate to capture Paris before the Americans got established over there. I'm sure the Americans had a profound influence on the outcome of the war.

After the Bolshevik Revolution we knew that eventually they would release hundreds of thousands of German troops. But we weren't bothered. Life was so precarious anyway, you only could live from day to day. You never thought, 'Well, in a few months' time they'll be after us,' because we didn't expect to live that long. The general strategy, if there was such a thing, seemed effective to us, but we knew nothing about it. We trusted our generals to a certain extent, but we really didn't know what was going on.

Life was so precarious anyway, you only could live from day to day.

DESERTION AND COWARDICE

Not all men wanted to fight. Some enlisted but found the stress of being at the front line unbearable; others had a moral objection to fighting and refused to join up. The punishment for either offence could be severe. During the Great War, 266 soldiers were executed by British Army firing squads for desertion and cowardice.

ABOVE: *A mother extolling her rather uncertain son to join up. These propaganda posters were extremely effective.*

Rifleman Henry Williamson
London Rifle Brigade

'WHILE I WAS AT ARMENTIÈRES I WAS DETAILED TO FORM PART OF A FIRING squad at the execution of a deserter. He was tied to a post against a wall in his civilian clothes, and we were told to fire at a piece of white cloth pinned over his heart. We didn't know what the rifles were loaded with – some were loaded with ball, others with blank. Then we had the order to fire and pulled the triggers – we knew by the recoil if it was loaded with ball or not. Then the deserter's name was read out on three successive parades, as a warning.'

Corporal Alan Bray

'ONE EVENING WHILE WE WERE IN THE TRENCHES AT ST ÉLOI I WAS warned that six of us had to go on a firing party to shoot four men of another battalion who had been accused of desertion. I was very worried about it because I didn't think it was right, in the first place, that Englishmen should be shooting other Englishmen. I thought we were in France to fight the Germans. Another reason was because I thought I knew why these men had deserted, if they had deserted. It was the fact that they had probably been in the trenches for two or three months without a break, which could absolutely break your nerve. So I really didn't feel like shooting them.

Anyway later in the evening an old soldier in another battery told me that it was the one thing in the Army that you could refuse to do. So I straightaway went back to the sergeant and said, 'I'm sorry, I'm not doing this,' and I heard no more about it.

I think one reason why I felt so strongly about it was the fact that the week before a boy in our own battalion had been shot for desertion. I knew that boy, and I knew that he absolutely lost his nerve, he couldn't have gone back into the line. Anyway he was shot, and the tragedy of it was that a few weeks later, in our local paper, I saw that his father had joined up to avenge his son's death on the Germans.'

Howard Marten
Conscientious objector

‘THE RANKS OF THE NO-CONSCRIPTION FELLOWSHIP WERE MADE UP OF men from every conceivable walk of life. You had all sorts of religious groups, from the Salvation Army to Seventh-Day Adventists, Church of England and Roman Catholics. Then you had the more politically minded: the Independent Labour Party and different degrees of Socialists. Then a very curious group of what I used to call the artistically minded – artists, musicians, all that. They had a terrific repugnance of war.

One or two of the officers and NCOs were quite reasonable men. There was a little Scottish regimental sergeant-major, and he almost had tears in his eyes. He said, 'You don't know what you're up against. You'll have an awful time.' He was genuinely concerned at the trouble that we were going to meet.

CONSCIENTIOUS OBJECTORS

A conscientious objector is a person who is opposed to serving in the armed forces or opposed to bearing arms for moral or religious principles. A group called the No-Conscription Fellowship was set up by conscientious objectors in 1914, to try to secure the legal right to exemption from military service. Any man who claimed this right was to be interviewed by a special panel, but in many cases their claims were turned down. Conscientious objectors were struck off the Electoral Roll for five years.

We were forever being threatened with the death sentence. Over and over again we'd be marched up and read out a notice: some man being sentenced to death through disobedience at the Front. Whether they were true cases I don't know. It was all done with the idea of intimidating us. But we wouldn't have taken that line unless we were prepared to face that situation, we realised that it was sufficiently serious.

We were forever being threatened with the death sentence.

Finally we had the second court martial, which took a whole day. It all had to be gone through all over again. Eventually we were taken out to the parade ground. There was a big concourse of men lined up in an immense square. Under escort we were taken out, one by one, to the middle of the square. I was the first of them, and until my verdict was known nobody knew exactly what was going to happen. Then the officer in charge of the proceedings read out the various crimes and misdemeanours – refusing to obey a lawful command, disobedience at Boulogne and so on. Then: 'The sentence of the court is to suffer death by being shot.'

There was a suitable pause, and I thought, 'Well, that's that.' Then he said, 'Confirmed by the Commander in Chief,' which double-sealed it. There was another long pause – 'But subsequently commuted to penal servitude for ten years.' And that was that. The thing that interested me particularly was that penal servitude meant your return to England, into the hands of the civil authorities at a civil prison.

It was all very strange. You had a feeling of being outside yourself, as if it wasn't affecting you personally, that you were just looking on at the proceedings. It was very curious.

RIGHT: *A clever propaganda poster shows a concerned mother with her daughter and young son, who is nevertheless convinced that either her husband or son should go and fight.*

E. J. Kealey
WOMEN OF BRITAIN
SAY –
"GO!"
Published by the PARLIAMENTARY RECRUITING COMMITTEE, London. Poster No. 75
Printed by HILL, SIFFKEN & Co. (L.P.A. Ltd.), Grafton Works, London, N. W. 13741 25 M. 3/15

ON THE HOME FRONT

With most of the young men away fighting, large numbers of women were called upon to help in the war effort. Many of them worked in munitions factories, making guns and filling and packing shells for the army.

Mrs M. Hall
Munitions worker

'I'D NEVER BEEN IN A FACTORY BEFORE, BUT THE CRISIS MADE YOU THINK. I thought well, my brothers and my friends are in France, so a friend and I thought to ourselves, well, let's do something. So we wrote to London and asked for war work. And we were directed to a munitions factory at Perivale in London. We had to have a health examination because we had to be very physically fit – perfect eyesight and strong. We had to supply four references, and be British-born of British parents.

ABOVE: *Female munitions workers checking shells.*
LEFT: *Women's Forestry Corps at work.*

We worked ten hours a day, that's from eight in the morning till quarter to one – no break, an hour for dinner, back again until half-past six – no break. We single girls found it very difficult to eat as well as work because the shops were closed when we got home. We had to do our work and try to get food, which was difficult. I remember going into a shop after not having milk for seven days and they said, 'If you can produce a baby you can have the milk' – that was it! I went into a butcher's shop to get some meat because we were just beginning to be rationed and I said, 'That looks like cat.' And he said, 'It is.' I couldn't face that.

It was a perfect factory to work in: everybody seemed unaware of the powder around them, unaware of any danger. Once or twice we heard, 'Oh, so and so's gone.' Perhaps she'd made a mistake and her eye was out, but there wasn't any big explosion during the three years I was there. We worked at making these little pellets, very innocent-looking little pellets, but had there been the slightest grit in those pellets, it would have been 'Goodbye'.

We had to do a fortnight on and a fortnight off. It was terribly hard, terribly monotonous, but we had a purpose. There wasn't a drone in that factory and every girl worked and worked and worked. I didn't hear one grumble and hardly ever heard of one that stayed home because she had her man in mind, we all had. I was working with sailors' wives from three ships that were torpedoed and sank, *Aboukir*, *Cressy* and *Hogue*, on the 22nd of September 1914. It was pitiful to see them, so we had to cheer them up as best we could, so we sang. It was beautiful to listen to.

After each day when we got home we had a lovely good wash. And believe me the water was blood-red and our skin was perfectly yellow, right down through the body, legs and toenails even, perfectly yellow. In some people it caused a rash and a very nasty rash all round the chin. It was a shame because we were a bevy

Yellow 'Canaries'

Working in a munitions factory was a dangerous job because the women were handling highly explosive chemicals, without much protection. One of these chemicals, sulphur, had a strange side effect. Those who worked with it found that their skin would turn yellow as it was gradually impregnated by the sulphur. The unusual colour of their face and hands earned them the nickname 'Canaries'.

of beauties, you know, and these girls objected very much to that. Yet amazingly even though they could do nothing about it, they still carried on and some of them with rashes about half an inch thick but it didn't seem to do them any inward harm, just the skin. The hair, if it was fair or brown it went a beautiful gold, but if it was any grey, it went grass-green. It was quite a twelve-month after we left the factory that the whole of the yellow came from our bodies. Washing wouldn't do anything – it only made it worse.

...we were such a happy band of women working amongst such treacherous conditions.

Each day we really and truly worked as I've never seen women work like it in my life before or since. It was just magic, we worked and we stood and we sat and we sang. If anyone had come into that factory they would never have believed it could have gone on, because we were such a happy band of women working amongst such treacherous conditions. **,**

Mabel Lethbridge
Munitions worker

' I WAS PUT INTO A SHELL-FILLING SHED WHERE I WAS TAUGHT TO FILL 18-pounder shells. We girls never went into a shed unless there were some of the older workers there to help us, but the older workers were always moaning. They were upset and miserable because there had been so many explosions, and I think they were justified, as we heard that machines we were going to be asked to work had been condemned.

We were continually searched for cigarettes, matches and anything you might have of metal. This went on hour after hour, you were continually pulled out for a search. There was a great feeling of tension all the time, although it was not exactly fear because we were very merry and always singing and very gay. The only difficulty I found when I was put on to one of these machines was that it was very tiring work. The shells were very heavy, and we had to kneel down in front of the machine. When you stood up you just felt you hadn't got any knees, and you hadn't got any back, except one aching mass. That was from all the carrying, the long hours and the weight. **,**

RIGHT: *A really powerful piece of propaganda aimed at women whose men had not enlisted.*

TO THE
YOUNG WOMEN OF LONDON

Is your "Best Boy" wearing Khaki? If not don't **YOU THINK** he should be?

If he does not think that you and your country are worth fighting for—do you think he is **WORTHY** of you?

Don't pity the girl who is alone—her young man is probably a soldier—fighting for her and her country—and for **YOU.**

If your young man neglects his duty to his King and Country, the time may come when he will **NEGLECT YOU.**

Think it over—then ask him to

JOIN THE ARMY TO-DAY

Mary Brough-Robertson
Munitions worker

, The most depressing thing about the war was the casualty lists. Every time you opened a paper it seemed to be nothing but casualty lists, and you always found people in them you knew. Then everybody wore black, and that was depressing too, black, black, black everywhere. Boys who came home didn't try and depress you, they tried to be as cheerful as they could. But they came home dirty and tired and wouldn't tell you much about anything, your own brothers wouldn't anyway. **,**

❝I WAS WORKING AS A VAD IN A HOSPITAL IN BULSTRODE STREET, IN West London. It was a big house taken over by the authorities, and all the cases were shell-shocked, which meant they couldn't keep their hands or their heads still. I had to hold them gently behind their heads and feed them, and I also used to write their love letters. Many couldn't say what they wanted to say, or they were probably too shy to tell me, but I used to write them for them, and let them read them back. I used to say, 'My dearest darling', you know, and 'Forever yours'.

I had to hold them gently behind their heads and feed them.

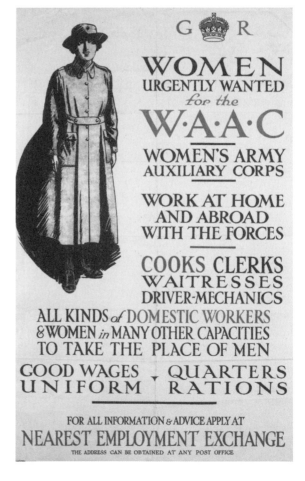

Heinrich Beutow
German schoolboy

❛BLACK-AND-WHITE POSTERS WENT UP SHOWING A MAN PUTTING A HAND to his lips and saying, 'Be careful, don't talk too much, the enemy is listening in.' Nobody took them very seriously. Not we as schoolchildren, anyway.

Food was getting scarce, queues were getting longer and soon going to a soup kitchen became one of the features of everyday life. Meat was particularly scarce. Butter was quite scarce and we had the famous German turnips again and again because there were so few potatoes. The winter of 1917 to 18 was called the Turnip Winter.

Schoolboys were taken out of school, and we had to go into houses and count everything – rabbits, for instance, and goats and sheep. Everybody seemed to be keeping rabbits because of the shortage of meat. Then they took us out in whole classes and sent us into the country to help the farmers. We liked that, but it meant we didn't get much teaching. All the teachers were out as soldiers anyway, and generally the whole life of the country was becoming grimmer.

There was a strong sense of people saying, 'This war is lasting too long.' Some became quite outspoken. The feeling was that the war was lasting too long and that Germany didn't have much chance of winning it, because the conditions within the country were getting so very difficult. ❜

There was a strong sense of people saying, 'This war is lasting too long.'

RIGHT: *British officers board a leave train on the Italian Front.*

TAKING LEAVE

Being sent home on leave was what

many soldiers dreamed of as they

endured months of living in the trenches.

But when the time came for them to go

home for a few days, many of them

found it hard to adjust to

normal civilian life.

Sergeant Jack Dorgan
7th Battalion, Northumberland Fusiliers

IN THE FIRST WEEK OF JUNE, ONLY ABOUT SIX OR SEVEN WEEKS AFTER we'd arrived in the trenches, the colonel sent for me. He said, 'Sergeant, this morning I've just received information from the War Office that leave can be started now. I've chosen you to be one of the first to go home to England for four days.' I came out of his dugout, took off my hat (steel helmets weren't invented then) put it on the bankside and put a bullet through it. I did it so that when I went home wearing a hat with a bullet hole through it, I could say, 'That was a near one.' And that's what I did.

Captain Charles Carrington
1/5th Battalion, Royal Warwickshire Regiment

‘ THIS WORLD OF THE TRENCHES, WHICH HAD BUILT UP FOR SO LONG AND which seemed to be going on forever, seemed like the real world, and it was entirely a man's world. Women had no part in it, and when one went on leave one escaped out of the man's world into the women's world. But one found that however pleased one was to see one's girlfriend, one could never somehow quite get through, however nice they were. If the girl didn't quite say the right thing one was curiously upset. One got annoyed by the attempts of well-meaning people to sympathise, which only reflected the fact that they didn't really understand at all. So there was almost a sense of relief when one went back into the man's world, which seemed the realest thing that could be imagined. ’

Mabel Lethbridge
Munitions worker

‘ WHEN MY FATHER AND BROTHERS, UNCLES, RELATIVES AND FRIENDS CAME home on leave and were staying at or visiting our house, I noticed a strange lack of ability to communicate with us. They couldn't tell us what it was really like. They would perhaps make a joke, but you'd feel it sounded hollow, as there was nothing to laugh about. They were restless at home, they didn't want to stay, they wanted to get back to the Front. They always expressed a desire to finish it. ’

LEFT: *September 1917 and British and Australian troops are jubilant on receiving their leave papers.*

They couldn't tell us what it was really like.

Lieutenant Edmund Blunden
11th Battalion, Royal Sussex Regiment

❝I BECAME INCREASINGLY UNCERTAIN OF THE VALUE OF RETURNING TO England for periods of leave. Of course being welcomed back and sitting down again with one's own, and going for a little trot and seeing a few people left whom one knew, that was a great thing. Yet not being able to discourse about the things which were at the forefront of one's feelings, that was difficult, and perhaps we had, over on the Western Front, placed too much emphasis on certain things.

I felt a little disconsolate after the first excitement of seeing everything in its usual corner. And then I didn't feel very happy about being treated as if I was a man of means because I had a uniform on. But it was chiefly that I felt I might as well not have been there, in all that muck, for all the notice that was paid to me.

Such was the attitude in England, but I ought to have known. It was everybody for himself in a way. And I suppose there was no reason why any one of us millions – because there were four million in Flanders and France in the end – why we should have been favoured with a nod and a bow and a 'Thank you very much', just for having got a bit muddier and more out of touch with good manners than we had been. ▌

Private Harold Carter

❝ I CAME HOME ON LEAVE FROM YPRES FOR FOUR DAYS. I GOT HOME, knocked at the door, and as they opened it I walked in and Mother rushed up as soon as she heard my voice. She was so pleased to see me she threw her arms round my neck and kissed me. Then she said, 'What's all this crawling about all over you?' I said, 'Well, mother, they're lice. Don't worry,' I said, but she was horrified. Of course, she never dreamt that conditions were such out there. I told her I'd have a wash down and dig out my civvy suit. Later on they asked me questions about what it was like over the other side but I didn't tell them too much. I didn't like to pile the agony on them at home. They knew that I'd had a rough time by looking at me – they didn't want telling twice. ▌

They knew that I'd had a rough time by looking at me – they didn't want telling twice.

THE U.S. MARINES

WANT YOU

APPLY AT

Fourth & Jefferson Sts., Louisville, Ky.

3

THE
FINAL
MONTHS

LEFT: *A naval recruitment poster urges American men to join up.
The arrival of American troops had a major impact on the Allies'
numbers and morale.*

ABOVE: *A jubilant young soldier returns from the Front.*

FIGHTING TO THE END

As the battle raged throughout the summer of 1918 it gradually became clear that the Allies were gaining the advantage. The effects of the Allied naval blockade and three years of fighting a war on two fronts had weakened the Germans considerably. For the Allies, fresh troops and new strategies proved a powerful combination.

ABOVE: *A soldier searching for a comrade's grave after the Battle of Pilckem Ridge, August 1917.*

BATTLE OF AMIENS

8 – 11 August 1918

On 8 August British Empire troops, spearheaded by Australians and Canadians, made a surprise attack on the German army. It was successful. Further Allied attacks during August forced the Germans, who had suffered heavy losses, to retreat. By 3 September they had been driven back to the Hindenburg Line, the starting point for their March 1918 attacks. The Allies had liberated much of German-occupied France and Belgium. By early October they broke through the Hindenburg Line into open country.

Private James Southey
Australian and New Zealand Army Corps

‘THE MORNING OF AUGUST THE 8TH STARTED VERY FOGGY INDEED, AND as our barrage opened, a tremendous barrage, we were wondering how we were going to get on. But, forward we pushed, and met comparatively slight opposition.

Some Germans surrendered quickly, others fought to the end. As we pushed on wondering where we were, the sun broke through and we began to see countryside that we hadn't seen for quite a time. It was unscarred, all sorts of cultivated land, and we began to feel, 'By Jove, the war's coming to an end. We're getting through.' And we had a feeling of great uplift about the whole job. **,**

THE BLACK DAY

One of the German commanders described 8 August 1918 as 'The Black Day of the German Army'. In the face of the British attack, German soldiers fled from the front and many of their units fell apart. Approximately 6,000 prisoners were taken and 100 artillery guns were seized. This success did not come without a cost for British troops, however, who also suffered heavy losses.

ABOVE: *For these German prisoners, the war is over as they are marched to captivity in August 1918.*

'In the summer of 1918 came the breakthrough. We had left the trenches behind, those mud-sodden trenches that we had hated for so many years. We were out in the open country. We almost felt victory in the air. Admittedly the Germans were standing and fighting here and there, but they were going back and we were following them. The breakthrough had come. It was open warfare. We were in green fields once again. However, open warfare brought its difficulties. This was the test of the trained soldier and junior officer leadership. The battalion commander had to watch his flanks, wondering when to stop, when to dig in, when to go on. We also had our ration problems. But it looked like the end and the peace we had longed for.'

The breakthrough had come. It was open warfare. We were in green fields once again.

Major S. Evers
Australian and New Zealand Army Corps

'We crossed the Somme marshes on the afternoon of the 31st of August and made our way to the place where we were supposed to be for the night. About midnight we had our meal and the shells were falling about there. In the complete darkness we were eating, eating dirt as well as food. About 2 o'clock we went to battalion headquarters, where a conference was held with candlelight. We were then given our dispositions where we were to attack at 6 o'clock. This meant time was getting very, very short indeed to get into position.

We wended our way as quickly as we could to the place where we were to meet our guides, who were to take us to the position where we were to attack. When we got there, there were no guides. But eventually we found our way to the front line into our trenches. Another company found Germans in their trench before, so had a sharp fight and ejected them. I sent a message to the OC [Officer Commanding] to say that I was in position. In the meantime the Germans must have sensed that we were coming over, because they put down a barrage of machine guns which were hitting the back of our trench with terrific thuds. It was a dreadful sound, and made more frightening because we knew that we'd have to get up and charge into it in a few minutes.

We'd advanced too far, so that the artillery did not know where our front line was, we wouldn't have any artillery to protect us when we launched our attack. I felt very much like refusing to allow the men to go over that morning, because it was sheer murder, but, of course, when the time came we had to do our duty and over the top we went. There were terrific casualties, men were going down right and left all over the place. I was with a sergeant-major just preparing to run from one position up forward when a machine-gun bullet got me through the thigh. I fell on the broad of my back and couldn't get up, the bullets were zipping all around me, and I could see over my toes the poor men of my company trying to get through the wire. Then the miracle happened, suddenly the Germans came out with their hands up! They were calling 'Kamerad'. All firing ceased. Had they fired for another few seconds, there wouldn't have been a man alive. That morning I went in with four officers and a hundred and eight men. By nightfall there were only eight men alive. But my remnant had joined up with B Company, passed through the wood, and had succeeded in capturing Péronne.

Then the miracle happened, suddenly the Germans came out with their hands up!

Those huge men, brave soldiers that they were, actually surrendered to the Australians.

The incredible surrender of the Germans at that moment was probably due to Private Currey who, under heavy machine-gun fire, killed the crew and captured single-handed a field gun which was holding up our advance. He then took out another post with a Lewis gun. He got a well-deserved VC. Another man, Crank, turned round a captured field gun and, at a range of two hundred yards, instead of the usual five or six hundred yards, fired directly into the German lines. That must have been the only reason why the Prussian Guard – who were the flower of the German Army – surrendered. They had volunteered to stay and protect that place at all costs because it was the last bastion before the Hindenburg Line. Those huge men, brave soldiers that they were, actually surrendered to the Australians.

Sergeant Melvin Krulewitch
United States Marine Corps

Every piece of artillery in the American Army and the adjoining French units opened up. This action produced a symphony in colour: you had the red artillery flares; orange flames coming out of the cannon; green signals

By early November the Allies were close to recapturing Mons, the place where the first British shots of the war had been fired in 1914. The fighting soon came to an end. Mons was finally taken on 11 November 1918, the day of the Armistice.

indicating possibility of gas attack, and you had the shells bursting in the air creating a white colour. On top of this you could hear the thunder of the guns. It was a great support to our morale to know that this extraordinary barrage was going on behind us. On we moved in the usual way, in a long skirmish line; men five yards apart, moving along at a leisurely pace, just making sure that you wouldn't get into our own barrage fire. The artillery fire had almost wiped out the first row of trenches, so we were soon in them and taking prisoners. One or two of our boys were wounded. A great shout of triumph went up and down the line when we made the German prisoners carry our wounded back on stretchers. Then we pushed ahead. Occasionally some of the boys would kneel and take a shot at a German, but they were retreating. Then another great shout of triumph went up because we'd captured their artillery: that was about two and a half miles behind the line.

We were attacked then by long-distance machine-gun fire and we had some casualties. The fire came from the heights of Bayonville, which was part of the Kriemhild Stellung defence line. That night we moved up and took the heights of Bayonville, so there was nothing ahead of us except the retreating Germans. And we pursued them relentlessly, night after night, day after day. The Germans were losing food; losing their artillery horses and their baggage and ration wagons. They were so hungry that they would shoot a horse and cut steaks out of the rump. At first we thought the horses had been hurt by shellfire: then we saw the skilful butchering of the steaks, and we knew what they had done. Finally we reached our objective, which was to cut the Metz–Malmédy railroad on the

It was a great support to our morale to know that this extraordinary barrage was going on behind us.

heights looking down to the Meuse River below Sedan. We cut that on the last night of the war – November 10th – and we put a footbridge across the Meuse River under withering gunfire. We crossed the river that night and made an attack on the other side. To us the fight was just like any other fight – the fight of the 9th, the 10th. That morning we found our wounded and gassed boys lying around on the ground and we took care of them. We expected an infantry attack, but the Germans never came that night, because there was too much gas in the woods and they took a chance of being killed themselves by their own gas if they attacked. So they let go with a box-barrage of the high-explosive shelling and mustard and phosgene gas. The following morning when we collected our unit, all I had was eleven men out of a company of over two hundred. *

They were so hungry that they would shoot a horse and cut steaks out of the rump.

BELOW: *German stretcher-bearers with Red Cross armbands, carrying a wounded British soldier during the early part of the Battle of the Somme.*

Herbert Sulzbach
9th Division, German Army

'In October I had leave to go home to Frankfurt, my home town, to my parents. I was very much looking forward to this leave after the terrific battles we had been through. I went through the streets of Frankfurt. I was not saluted. I was a commissioned offficer, yet no one saluted. Everything was rationed and there was hardly anything to buy. Dance halls were closed, the streets were dull and the mood of the people was really bad. We hadn't realised at the Front how bad it was at home. People were fed up with war. They wanted the war to be ended as soon as possible, victory or no victory. After a fortnight I went back to the front line, to my comrades, to my guns, and I felt at home amongst the mud, the dirt and the lice.

In spite of our retreats for weeks and months, we still received mail, bags of it, even some with parcels. Parcels didn't come from Germany but from Belgium, where there was still some food and chocolate. The letters I received were not depressing, but some of my comrades received letters which were most upsetting. Their families wrote, 'We have nothing to eat, we are fed up with war, come back as soon as possible.' You can imagine how it affected the morale of these poor chaps.

On November the 1st we were at Étreux not far from St Quentin, where we had started our big offensive on March the 21st. Then we were so full of hope and broke through the British 5th Army. Now it seems a million guns of the American, French and British were bombing us. The war was entirely lost. As adjutant I had to give the order of the day. On the 11th of November it was: 'From noon onwards our guns will be silent.' Four years before, full of optimism, now a beaten army.'

RIGHT: *Winchester Cathedral, where men of the United States Army pay tribute to their fallen comrades.*

ARMISTICE

Germany's kaiser abdicated and fled Germany on 9 November. Two days later Germany signed the terms of surrender. It was a historic moment – the fighting ended at 11 am on the 11th day of the 11th month, 1918. The exhausted armies stopped fighting and finally there was quiet on the Western Front.

ABOVE: *The day the world had waited for – the Armistice.*

RIGHT: *Casualties being cared for aboard a moored barge.*

Marine Hubert Trotman
Royal Marine Light Infantry

'WE WERE STILL FIGHTING HARD AND LOSING MEN. WE KNEW NOTHING of the proposed Armistice, we didn't know until a quarter to ten on that day. As we advanced on the village of Guiry a runner came up and told us that the Armistice would be signed at 11 o'clock that day, the 11th of November. That was the first we knew of it.

We were lined up on a railway bank nearby, the same railway bank that the Manchesters had lined up on in 1914. They had fought at the Battle of Mons in

August that year. Some of us went down to a wood in a little valley and found the skeletons of some of the Manchesters still lying there. Lying there with their boots on, very still, no helmets, no rusty rifles or equipment, just their boots. ’

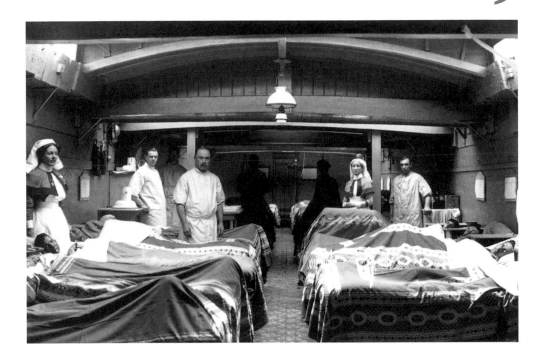

Major Keith Officer
Australian and New Zealand Army Corps

‘At 11 o’clock on the 11th of November I was sitting in a room, in the Brewer’s House at Le Cateau, which had been Sir John French’s headquarters at the time of the battle of Mons. I was sitting at a table with a major in the Scots Greys who had a large, old-fashioned hunting watch which he put on the table and watched the minutes going round. When 11 o’clock came, he shut his watch up and said, ‘I wonder what we are all going to do next!’ That was very much the feeling of everyone. What was one going to do next? To some of us it was the end

of four years, to others three years, to some less. For many of us it was practically the only life we had known. We had started so young.

Nearby there was a German machine-gun unit giving our troops a lot of trouble. They kept on firing until practically 11 o'clock. At precisely 11 o'clock an officer stepped out of their position, stood up, lifted his helmet and bowed to the British troops. He then fell in all his men in the front of the trench and marched them off. I always thought that this was a wonderful display of confidence in British chivalry, because the temptation to fire on them must have been very great.

Corporal Clifford Lane
1st Battalion, Hertfordshire Regiment

AS FAR AS THE ARMISTICE ITSELF WAS CONCERNED, IT WAS A KIND OF anticlimax. We were too far gone, too exhausted really, to enjoy it. All we wanted to do was go back to our billets, there was no cheering, no singing. That day we had no alcohol at all. We simply celebrated the Armistice in silence and thankfulness that it was all over. And I believe that happened quite a lot in France. It was such a sense of anticlimax. We were drained of all emotion. That's what it amounted to. '

Sergeant-Major Richard Tobin
Hood Battalion, Royal Naval Division

'THE ARMISTICE CAME, THE DAY WE HAD DREAMED OF. THE GUNS STOPPED, the fighting stopped. Four years of noise and bangs ended in silence. The killings had stopped.

We were stunned. I had been out since 1914. I should have been happy. I was sad. I thought of the slaughter, the hardships, the waste and the friends I had lost. '

ABOVE: *Two members of the Women's Auxiliary Army Corps attend the graves of fallen British soldiers at Abbeville in February 1918.*

FIRST WORLD WAR TIMELINE

This timeline shows some of the key events and major battles of the First World War, focusing on the Western Front.

28 June
Archduke Franz Ferdinand is assassinated.

28 July
Austria–Hungary declares war on Serbia.

1 August
Germany declares war on Russia.

3 August
Germany declares war on France.

4 August
Britain declares war on Germany. The Germans advance in the West through Belgium.

5 August
Austria–Hungary declares war on Russia.

6 August
Serbia declares war on Germany.

12 August
Britain and France declare war on Austria–Hungary.

23 August
The Battle of Mons – the first major British battle of the First World War – begins.
Japan declares war on Germany.

23 – 31 August
The Germans defeat the Russians at the Battle of Tannenberg, in East Prussia.

5 – 9 September
First Battle of the Marne, in which the German advance on the Western Front is halted. A 'race to the sea' follows.

5 - 15 September
The Germans defeat the Russians at Masurian Lakes, East Prussia.

12 - 15 September
Battle of the Aisne marks the beginning of trench warfare.

19 October
First Battle of Ypres begins. Trench system begins to be established.

29 October
Turkey joins the Central Powers.

2 November
Russia declares war on Turkey.

5 November
Britain and France declare war on Turkey.

LEFT: *This American poster uses persuasion techniques to boost naval recruitment.*

1915
4 February – 19 December

1916
21 February – 7 December

4 February
Germany announces unrestricted submarine warfare to blockade Britain, beginning on 18 February.

10 – 13 March
Battle of Neuve Chapelle takes place.

18 March
Allied naval forces fail to pass through the Dardanelles.

22 April – 25 May
Second Battle of Ypres. Poison gas used by the Germans for the first time.

25 April
Allied forces land on the Gallipoli Peninsula, Turkey.

7 May
The British passenger ship, *Lusitania*, carrying a number of American citizens, is torpedoed and sunk by the Germans.

23 May
Italy declares war on Austria–Hungary.

5 August
The Germans capture Warsaw, Poland.

25 September – 8 October
First Battle of Loos.

11 October
Bulgaria joins the Central Powers.

19 December
British forces begin their withdrawal from the Gallipoli Peninsula.

21 February
The Germans launch an offensive at Verdun.

24 April
Easter uprising against British rule in Ireland.

31 May – 1 June
British and German fleets clash at sea in the Battle of Jutland.

1 July
Battle of the Somme begins.

27 August
Romania joins the Allies.

31 August
Battle of Verdun ends.

September
The Germans begin to build the Hindenburg Line.

15 September
Tanks used by British forces for the first time in battle.

18 November
Battle of the Somme ends.

7 December
David Lloyd George succeeds Asquith as British Prime Minister.

1917
15 March – 15 December

15 March
Czar Nicholas II of Russia abdicates.

6 April
The United States declares war on Germany.

18 July
Germans defeat Russians at Eastern Front. Russia is in no state to fight on.

31 July
Third Battle of Ypres begins. Also known as the 'Passchendaele offensive'.

7 November
Bolshevik revolution in Russia. Lenin comes to power and takes Russia out of the war.

10 November
Third Battle of Ypres ends. The village of Passchendaele is taken by the British.

20 November
Battle of Cambrai. First successful tank battle for the British.

7 December
United States declares war on Austria–Hungary.

15 December
Central Powers and Russia begin peace negotiations.

1918
3 March – 11 November

3 March
Russia and the Central Powers sign peace treaty.

21 March – May
Germans advance on the Western Front, breaking through the British lines.

June – July
Allies fight back.

18 July – 7 August
Second Battle of the Marne.

August
Allies advance and German morale begins to crack.

8 – 11 August
Battle of Amiens.

September – October
Allies break through the Hindenburg Line.

19 – 25 September
Turks defeated by British at Megiddo.

30 September
Bulgaria signs armistice with Allies.

30 October
Turkey signs armistice with Allies.

3 November
Austria–Hungary signs armistice with Allies.

9 November
Kaiser Wilhelm II of Germany abdicates.

11 November
Armistice is signed between the Allies and Germany. The fighting ends.

Military Ranks in the British Army During the First World War

The list begins with the highest military rank and goes down, rank by rank, to the lowest.

Field Marshal
General
Lieutenant-General
Major-General
Brigadier-General
Colonel
Lieutenant-Colonel
Major
Captain

Lieutenant
2nd Lieutenant

Sergeant-Major
Sergeant
Corporal
Lance-Corporal
Private

First World War Statistics

No-one is sure exactly how many servicemen were killed in action in the First World War. Here are the approximate figures for the countries that fought in the war:

War Deaths

Allies

Russia 1,700,000

France & its colonies 1,400,000

Britain 745,000

 Her Empire: India 72,000
    Australia 60,000
    New Zealand 17,000
    South Africa 6,000
    Canada 56,500
    Newfoundland 2,000

Italy 650,000

Romania 335,000

United States 116,000

Serbia 48,000

Belgium 14,000

Portugal 7,000

Greece 5,000

Japan 300

Central Powers

Germany 1,800,000

Austro–Hungarian Empire 1,200,000

Turkey 325,000

Bulgaria 87,000

GLOSSARY

AGUE a feverish chill, causing shaking fits

ALLIES name given to France, Britain, Russia, Serbia, Italy, Japan and Romania (the United States was an Associated Power)

AMMUNITION supplies of bullets and shells

ARMISTICE an agreement to stop fighting

ARTILLERY heavy guns such as cannons, also the name for the military units that use them, e.g. Royal Artillery

ASSASSINATION the murder of a person, usually for political reasons

BALACLAVA a knitted woollen 'helmet', worn over the head to keep out the cold

BARRAGE concentrated artillery bombardment

BATTALION a unit of roughly 850 soldiers, forms part of a regiment

BATTERY the place where a piece of artillery is positioned

BAYONET a long, sharp metal blade attached to a rifle

BILLY CAN a small metal cooking pot

'BLIGHTY ONE' a wound that would get the soldier back to 'Blighty' (slang for Britain)

BLOCKADE blocking a country, usually with ships, to prevent supplies reaching it

'BOCHE' slang word for a German soldier

BOMBARDMENT heavy, concentrated shelling by the artillery

BRITISH EXPEDITIONARY FORCE (BEF) the army of regular soldiers and reservists who were the first British troops to fight in Belgium in 1914

BUNKER an underground shelter

CALL-UP an official summons to do military service

CAMOUFLAGE to blend in with the background – army uniforms are usually camouflaged to conceal the soldier in his environment

CAVALRY soldiers on horseback

CENTRAL POWERS name given to Germany, Austria–Hungary, Bulgaria and Turkey

CIVILIAN a person who is not a soldier

'CIVVY' SUIT clothes worn by civilians or troops on leave ('civvy' is short for 'civilian')

CONSCIENTIOUS OBJECTOR a person who refuses to take part in military service or bear arms on the grounds of religious or moral principles

CONSCRIPTION a law that states men of certain ages must do military service

COURT MARTIAL a military court that tries people for offences under military law

DARDANELLES the southernmost end of the sea passage from the Aegean to the Black Sea

DIRK a Scottish dagger

DUCKBOARD wooden slats laid over muddy ground in a trench

EASTERN FRONT the battle front between Russia and the Central Powers in Eastern Europe

ENFILADE gunfire directed along the entire flank of a target, such as a column of troops

ENLIST to enrol in the army willingly

ESTAMINET small French café

FLANK the left or right side of an army

HINDENBURG LINE the line of trench systems established in 1917 that were the last and strongest of the German army's defence on the Western Front

HOWITZER a gun that fired heavy shells, which seemed to come down almost vertically

INFANTRY foot soldiers

INSIGNIA a badge of office or rank

'JERRY' slang word for a German soldier

'JOCK' slang word for a Scot

KAISER WILHELM II the Emperor of
Germany, also known as 'Kaiser Bill'

'KAMERAD' German for 'comrade'

LATRINE a communal toilet, often just a pit
dug in the ground

LEWIS GUN a type of British machine gun
(invented by an American)

LUGER PISTOL a small hand-held German gun

MAGAZINE a stock of ammunition or a
compartment for ammunition in a firearm

MILLS BOMB a type of hand grenade

MOBILISATION the immediate preparation of
troops for war

MUNITIONS weapons and military equipment

NO MAN'S LAND the name given to the area
between the two front lines, which neither
side controlled

OTTOMAN EMPIRE Turkish Muslim empire
that once ruled large parts of the Middle
East and the Balkans

PATRIOTISM love of one's own country

POILU slang word for a French soldier in the
infantry

PROPAGANDA information (sometimes false)
that is given out to influence people's opinions,
often used by governments during wars

REDOUBT a small protected place of shelter or
defence

REGIMENT a military unit consisting of at least
two battalions

RESERVISTS men who are not regular soldiers
but who have some training and are ready to
fight if necessary

SANDBAG a sack filled with sand, used to make
protective walls at the sides of the trenches
in the war

SENTRY a guard

SHELL an explosive that is fired by an artillery
gun

SHELL SHOCK a name given to a stress-related
mental illness that soldiers often suffered
from, either during combat or on their return

SHRAPNEL fragments of an exploded bomb,
mine or shell

SNIPER a person who fires shots from a
concealed position

SQUADRON a unit of ten to eighteen military
planes

SUBALTERN a Second Lieutenant

'TOMMY' slang word for a British soldier

TRENCH a deep ditch dug in the ground

TRUCE a temporary agreement between
enemies to stop fighting

VICTORIA CROSS (VC) Britain's highest
military award for bravery

VOLUNTARY AID DETACHMENTS (VAD)
female volunteers who helped provide
medical assistance during the war

WESTERN FRONT the front line of the First
World War in Western Europe, running
through France and Belgium

'WHIZZ-BANG' a small high-velocity shell that
made a whizzing sound, followed by a loud
explosion

ZOUAVE an Algerian soldier serving with the
French army

FINDING OUT MORE ABOUT THE FIRST WORLD WAR

The First World War is a fascinating subject and there are many resources available for you to use to discover more about different aspects of the war. You should be able to find a range of books in your local or school library that will tell you about the history and background in more detail. Many films, documentaries and television series have been made on this subject over the years and you may be able to borrow these on video or DVD, also from the library. Some well-known films are *All Quiet on the Western Front* (1930), *Dawn Patrol* (1938), *Lawrence of Arabia* (1962) and *Gallipoli* (1981).

There are many hundreds of eyewitness accounts from the First World War. A wonderfully varied selection of these accounts can be found in the book and the CD *Forgotten Voices of the Great War* by Max Arthur, the source for the stories contained in this edition.

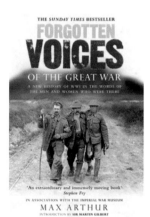

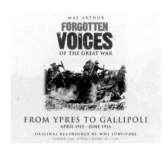

There is a wealth of poetry that was written by those who experienced the Great War. Wilfred Owen, Siegfried Sassoon and Rupert Brooke are some of the most famous war poets.

The Internet contains a great deal of information about the war. Here are some good websites to browse:

www.firstworldwar.com
www.nationalarchives.gov.uk/pathways/firstworldwar
www.schoolshistory.org.uk
www.bbc.co.uk/schools/worldwarone
www.bbc.co.uk/history/war/wwone
www.spartacus.schoolnet.co.uk
www.channel4.com/history/microsites/F/firstworldwar

About the Imperial War Museum

Imperial War Museum London

Packed with fascinating exhibits and amazing facts, this museum tells the story of what life was like in the front line and on the home front during both World Wars. Visitors can experience the drama of an air raid, complete with sounds, smells and special effects, walk through a re-creation of a First World War trench, find out about evacuees and rationing, and discover the undercover world of wartime espionage.

Churchill Museum and Cabinet War Rooms

Concealed beneath the streets of Westminster, the Cabinet War Rooms was Winston Churchill's secret underground headquarters during the Second World War. Visitors can see where Churchill worked, ate and slept, protected from the bombing raids above, and discover more about the life of this extraordinary man in the Churchill Museum.

HMS Belfast

The museum's third London branch is a Second World War ship moored on the River Thames near the Tower of London. It gives a unique insight into naval history and the harsh, dangerous conditions which her crew endured. Visitors can explore nine decks to find out what life was like when living and working on board a warship.

All sorts of interactive family activities take place throughout the year at every branch of the Imperial War Museum. These range from code-breaking activities to art and sculpture sessions and the chance to handle wartime artefacts as well as opportunities to meet veterans and find out first-hand what life was like during wartime.

Imperial War Museum Duxford

Based near Cambridge, this is one of the country's biggest air museums, sited on a former Battle of Britain station. It has a unique collection including biplanes, Spitfires, Concorde and Gulf War jets. During the summer, many of these legendary aircraft take to the sky for Duxford's world-class airshows.

Imperial War Museum North

The museum's newest branch in Manchester is housed in an unusual and dramatic building representing conflict on land, sea and air. This museum offers exhibitions, family events and a dynamic audio-visual show called the Big Picture.

For further information about the Imperial War Museum visit: www.iwm.org.uk

INDEX OF CONTRIBUTORS

GENERAL INDEX

Page numbers in italic refer to the illustrations

PHOTOGRAPHIC CREDITS

All photography and illustrations © Imperial War Museum. p.5 IWM PST 5277; p.6 IWM PST
10481; p.10 IWM PST 13167, p.14 Q 88541; p.15 Q49369; p.17 Q 58482; p.18 Q 53; p.19 Q
33176; p.21 Q 30 686; p.22 IWM PST 0243; p.23 IWM PST 0318; p.24 Q 81730; p.25 Q 30060;
p.27 Q 81778; p.28 SR 68; p.29 IWM PST 2734; p.30 Q 30066; p.31 Q 81797; p.33 IWM PST
2734; p.34 Q 81785; p.40 IWM REPRO 000681; p.42 Q 81781; p.44 Q 53305; p.46 Q 51486; p.47
MH 6561; p.48 Q 51506; p.52 Q 51489; p.53 Q 50720; p.55 Q 469; p.56 IWM PST 10481; p.57 Q
3987; p.59 Q 10686; p.62 Q 4665; p.64 SR 314; p.65 Q 3121; p.70 Q 6595; p.72 IWM ART 1460;
p.74 Q 48951; p.75 Q 114867; p.78 Q 29001; p.81 Q 103291; p.85 Q 70701; p.86 Q 13633; p.89 Q
53; p.90 Q 912; p.94 Q 2486 ; p.97 Q 6224; p.98 SR 11; p.99 Q 2855; p.100 Q 2265; p.103 Q 6050;
p.104 Q 23804; p.106 Q 6279; p.107 Q 1872; p.109 Q 42255; p.113 Q 68852; p.115 IWM PST
0351; p.117 SR 33; p.119 IWM PST 2763; p.120 Q 30705; p.121 Q 30018; p.124 IWM PST 4903;
p.125 IWM PST 13171; p.127 Q25794; p.128 Q3096; p.130 Q 30402; p.132 IWM PST 0274;
p.133 Q 2689; p.135 Q2756; p.136 C.O 2988; p.141 Q 760; p.143 Q 31231; p.145 Q 33443; p.146
Q 3365; p.147 Q 847; p.148 IWM PST 0246.